The Gift *of* Desperation

The True Story of God's Grace Alive in a Life

KATE JANSON

www.godsgracealiveinalife.com

Cover Design: Oladimeji Alaka

Editing and Page Design: Ashley Hagan @Inkwellwriters.com

Paperback ISBN: 9798218530136
eBook ISBN: 9798218537371

Quotations marked *Alcoholics Anonymous* are taken from W., Bill. *Alcoholics Anonymous: The Story of How Many Thousands of Men and Women Have Recovered from Alcoholism*. New York: Alcoholics Anonymous World Services, 2002.

For it is by grace you have been saved, through faith — and this is not from yourselves, it is the gift of God — not by works, so that no one can boast.

Ephesians 2:8-9

I dedicate this book--which is my life--to God the Father, God the Son, and God the Holy Spirit. He created me in my mother's womb and had a plan for my life, as He does with all of our lives. If He can save a wretch like me, He can save anyone. If you don't know Him, I pray this book will encourage you to seek Him and know the love that will be your source of comfort through the storms of life.

TABLE OF CONTENTS

Chapter 1

THE CORNERSTONE

My story is about the miracle of God doing the impossible! It is a story of God's grace alive in a life. When I came to the end of myself, I could no longer hide from the pain of the broken life I had been living. I was desperate to stop the noise in my head that told me I was worthless, unforgivable, and had nothing to offer anyone. My desperate attempts at making the right decisions were always sabotaged with chaos and destruction by my own hand. I became more and more isolated because I was filled with such shame and self-hate that it was easier to not show up for life than it was to face my friends and family while trying to hide the hopelessness I felt. When I finally cried out to God for help, I had no more "good ideas" of how to fix myself. I surrendered!

"The stone the builders rejected has become the cornerstone; the Lord has done this, and it is marvelous in our eyes. The Lord has done it this very day; let us rejoice today and be glad."
Psalm 118:22-24

"'Do I now believe, or am I even willing to believe, that there is a Power greater than myself?' As soon as a man can say that he does believe, or is willing to believe, we emphatically assure him that he is on his way. It has been repeatedly proven among us that upon this simple cornerstone a wonderfully effective spiritual structure can be built."
Alcoholics Anonymous, pg. 47
(also known as the "Big Book")

Why is this correlation so important? God took all the struggles, addiction, and loss of my life and made beauty from ashes. Sinful actions were turned to useful tools. As humans, we carry this belief that if God is a righteous judge, then we will be burning in Hell. The truth, in its simplistic form, is that the journey of the relationship with God is truly a love story. I was independently trying to live my life and fell prey to my alcoholism. Instead of rejecting me in my choices, God stayed with me, loved me, and sent His angels charge over me while I was in the throes of the hell of my addiction. My story shows how the love of the Lord took my broken life and carried me, healed me, and gave me a purpose.

"But because of His great love for us, God, who is rich in mercy, made us alive with Christ even when we were dead in transgressions—it is by grace you have been saved!"
Ephesians 2:4-5

It was a simple purpose, but never would I have imagined that through the depths of my worst self, my simple purpose would be the greatest tool, allowing me to help others with my experience, strength, and hope. Only God would take the underbelly of my life that I wanted to keep in the dark and use it as a beacon of hope for the women who were stuck in the dark. Through my journey of healing, I was able to develop a strength with my faith in Him to live life like a loose garment—free from being controlled by what other people thought of me. I could weather the storms because He was my shield. He was my protector. How did I know this? Because I wasn't angry, I wasn't bitter, and I knew He was with me. I knew I could trust him with my loved ones as well. I trusted that He was caring for them because I asked Him to and because He loved them way more than I could. He was their loving God as well. The only difference between me and the person who feels alone and scared is faith. That's why I pray that anyone who is searching for comfort in this scary world or feels as though their past or future is too much for them would understand there is no hope when they believe their purpose is only slogging on to the bitter end and hoping for the best. Why wouldn't God have a better purpose for you? If you believe with only a mustard seed of faith that a loving God created you and that Jesus died on the cross, then your purpose is much better than that no-hope existence.

You may be going about your life just doing whatever you think is right. Maybe life has been "just fine," but you still struggle with fear and having no sense of purpose. If that's the case, you are missing out on the one relationship that will fill that missing piece of your soul, the one you're always trying to get beyond.

How could a judging God bless me with grace and mercy? After reading my story, you still might wonder why He would bless me. I certainly didn't deserve it based on my merits. Why would He materialize the whispers of my heart and choose me to help others who are dying from the deadly disease of alcoholism? Why would He allow me to help them build the life that He designed for them? Why would He bless me with children when I aborted mine? The answer is because the WHOLE purpose of God the Father, the Son, and the Holy Spirit is LOVE!

Making time to read and study the Bible isn't lame like I once thought it was; it's an adventure! You may have heard Christians say the Bible is "alive," and it is. It is also pertinent to your struggles, your fears, your hurts, your direction, your protection, and your purpose. But you have to first believe that it holds truth for your life. The circumstances shown in the Bible may be different from yours in their details, but the feelings are the same. When you read the Bible with that in mind, expecting it to contain answers and truth, then the characters come to life. You see yourself as a David fighting the Goliaths in your life; or Mary Magdalene, controlled by the addictions in your life; or Peter who denied Christ three times. I said no so many times to knowing God or trying to have a relationship with God, but He was patiently right there. I had to step out in courage "for such a time as this" (Esther 4:14).

God is waiting for you to invite Him into your life. He is loving you and sending His angels charge over you. Search for the comfort and love of God in any and all ways, for it is the key to filling that round hole you have tried to fill with a square block. When you do, you will feel a peace and comfort beyond your understanding in any and all circumstances. I pray that for you.

> *"May God bless you and keep you.*
> *May He make His face shine upon*
> *you and be gracious to you. May He*
> *turn His face towards you and give*
> *you peace!"*
> Numbers 6:24-26

It takes a faith that only comes from experience after experience of witnessing God show up mightily when it seemed like there was no hope, things were impossible to overcome, or the worst set of circumstances were about to unfold. God gives a kiss on the cheek that is felt in ways that are incomprehensible, and I fall to my knees in gratitude. It is what I need to take God's direction each day without knowing the outcome.

Obedience is not my strong suit, but my faith and willingness to follow God's direction, despite my willful self-desire, has always proved to be a blessing on the other side of the character-building path He has placed me on. I remind myself of the honor He has bestowed on me—a modern day Mary Magdalene—to help other people who are hurting find the hope of forgiveness, healing, and transformation. If it has been bestowed on me, it certainly will be a gift to you.

God's story of redemption in my life is a "long and windy road" that is blessed and broken, blessed and broken. God carefully has the guardrails up for each hairpin turn to prevent me from falling off the cliff.

Chapter 2

THE INNOCENCE

Do you remember summer days as a little one lying on the grass looking up at the sky? Close your eyes; imagine yourself lying there. The sun was warm on your face, the wind blew gently . . . not a care in the world. If you looked over to the left or to the right, you were eye level with the grass. Watching a ladybug crawl up the blade, you would put your finger out, and she would crawl on your hand until it was time to fly away. I would spend hours in my backyard doing all of those things. It was a simple, gentle, carefree time. My mind was free to just BE!

My first memory of my relationship with God was during this time. I was lying in the grass looking at the clouds, and I saw a vision. I saw a chariot and horses, and Jesus was in the chariot. Angels were all around, dressed like warriors with massive wings. Oh, what a sight it was! I don't remember being afraid at all; I felt comforted knowing it will be so exciting when He comes to earth. The innocence of my faith at that time obviously couldn't comprehend all that would come with His promised return. I just had the childlike faith that He was coming.

"They will see the Son of Man
coming on the clouds of heaven with
power and great glory. And He will
send out His angels with a loud
trumpet call, and they will gather
His elect from the four winds, from
one end of heaven to the other."
Matthew 24:30-31

The other thing I remember as a "wee one" was telling my mother "I was forgetting" what it was like to be in heaven. OK?? I might have lost you right there, however, it is unusual for me to still have those memories at sixty-something years old. CRAZY . . . I'll let you decide.

Raised Catholic, I went to church every Sunday. There was no Sunday School, so we children attended the full service. I was a handful, to say the least: a curly-top, red-headed toddler filled with boundless joy. Sounds delightful, but not so easy to handle in settings that required composure. Not my strong suit. I had three older brothers, and the youngest of the three was seven years older than me. Then I came along—I must note that my parents never said I was anything but a blessing, the little girl they prayed for. However, you can't miss that I probably wasn't in their original long-term plan. My birth was followed shortly by my baby brother because they wanted to make sure I had a playmate.

I can remember my mother putting my hair in "pin curls" for church, and she would say this little ditty:

"There was a little girl who had a little curl
Right in the middle of her forehead.
And when she was good she was very, very good,
But when she was bad, she was horrid."

Well, the "horrid" part came later. Up until first grade, I always tried to be the perfect little Catholic girl. I tried as hard as I could not to get into trouble. But then, not getting into trouble became more important than being truthful and getting into trouble. Unfortunately, that thinking is one of the things that led me down the path of destruction. I can remember wanting to be perfect in following the Ten Commandments, but then I would lie because I was going to get into trouble . . . the end of the innocence. It was the little things, like stealing my mom's M&M's. Not the whole bag, just a few in the bag. Or sneaking food when my mom or my brothers weren't around (chocolate chips dipped in peanut butter). It all went south from there.

Life was simple then. I grew up in the 1960s and 70s. There was a lot of political change going on, but I never really experienced it. I was too busy playing outside. I was born in Utica, New York, and it was a day and age where, as children, you left the house in the morning and played with your friends all day, only coming back for meals. When my mother would want us to come home for dinner, she would ring a cowbell. You could hear it through the neighborhood. We had a lot of children in the neighborhood. We would play games in the backyard—everyone's backyard. We would roll down the hill for hours, swing on the swing set, climb in the ravine, ride our bikes. The freedom and safety we felt! Everyone took care of each other. If you fell off your bike up the street, one of the moms would clean you up and send you on your way.

My parents instilled in my brother and me a sense of service. My mother always brought my younger brother Peter and me everywhere with her. She was always a dutiful daughter and friend. We would clean the lake house in the spring, we would go to my grandparents' house in Amsterdam, New York, to visit and help when my Nana had a stroke, making meals or cleaning the house for my grandfather. Then we would visit my grandfather when my grandmother passed away.

Through it all, God blessed me with a buoyant spirit, which was one of light, joy, and laughter, designed to shine the Lord's light in this world. I was filled with vim and vigor as a young child, dancing and singing as I went about my very middle-class existence, just taking in all the beauty. I found such joy in the simple things: a song on the radio, the first snowfall, Santa Claus. My eyes would well with emotion; it was all magical and wonderful! I would sing songs and want to twirl and twirl until I fell down. I loved it when the kids in the neighborhood would come over and roll down the hill into the neighbor's yard, day after day. It was innocent fun, and we would laugh until our belly hurt. I loved to have everyone in my backyard. It was such a time of innocence! We would go to "the ravine," which was a whole magical world of exploration. We would scale down the side of the ravine and look for toads and salamanders. It was an adventure every time.

But for some reason, my sweet little spirit never really felt like I fit in. Because I had red hair, the kids on the street would sometimes call me Carrot Top, which made me feel different, and it hurt that they would call me names. When I felt like they were being mean to me, I would run home to my mother, and they would make fun of that as well. My mother was a remarkable woman who managed five children, kept the house, taught physical education, and always had dinner on the table at seven o'clock after "treat" and the news. "Treat" was what my parents called their six o'clock relaxing time. When she was home, she was busy just trying to keep the house together and the boys out of mischief. With tears streaming down my face, I would ask, "Why don't they like me? Why are they so mean?" Those were the first of many punches my sweet spirit took from the enemy in his effort to steal my joy, my confidence, and my trust in the Lord.

My mom would continue to cook in the kitchen while telling me, "They are just jealous, dear. Now go back out and play." When you were little in the 60s, Mom didn't come rescue you. I learned at an early age to push down my feelings, pull up my "Big Girl Panties," and go back into the ring. I learned how to manage uncomfortable feelings like fear and disappointment by having to go back into the very environment that made me feel unwanted or less than and try again. The problem was, I had no guidance or wisdom directing me. Although my mother was able to handle a lot, I think she stepped into survival mode with three teenage boys, raging in hormones, in a house with one bathroom for seven people. Need I say more?

My father was raised with all brothers, then had three sons. He was not equipped to raise a little girl, especially a vivacious, little, curly-top redhead. Since no one in my family could see beyond their own circle of life, my challenge was to figure out how to get people to like me, even with my red hair.

Chapter 3

THE BLESSING OF A LIFETIME

God's grace was all over me as a sweet little cherub; my spirit couldn't be broken, as hard as the enemy tried. This is one of the sweetest blessings from the Lord, a buoyant spirit! You may think, "Well, that's not much of a blessing," but His gifts are not always a gift that is material or one that fixes the immediate uncomfortable situation (although that can happen as well). In hindsight, I found myself with a blessing that is far greater than a material one. The ability to overcome life struggles by picking myself up and brushing myself off has been such a gift in navigating life's ups and downs. It was like building an arsenal of tools that would lead me to the life He had for me. I believe he laid the groundwork and put all the pieces in place.

Since the children on the street never made me feel a part of them, my tender spirit always felt separated and alone. God has provided for me every need that was essential to living out His calling on my life. Of course, I didn't recognize it at such a young age, but He knew I would need more than a friend on the street. Instead, He blessed me with a soulmate for a lifetime. He brought me my beautiful cousin, who has been my favorite person in the world my whole life. My mother had only one sister, my Aunt Teresa, and she had four children. The youngest was a pretty, blonde-haired, blue-eyed, kind, thoughtful, creative, sensitive, and very witty girl named Grace. I was the outgoing one while Grace was the shy one. I would see Grace only once a year, but we had a connection that was of divine affinity. My mother and her sister had a family lake house which our grandparents built in the 1930s. As the sisters grew up, they would leave their residence on State Street in Albany, NY, and summer on Glass Lake, which was about thirty minutes outside Albany. When the sisters got married and had families of their own, my grandparents split the summer into two months, with our family vacationing in the month of July and the Huberts (my Aunt Teresa's family) vacationing in August. August was the horse racing season, and my aunt and uncle loved the racetrack, so we would always go with them to the races at Saratoga Race Track in Saratoga Springs, New York.

When it was the end of July, our month for vacation ended and overlapped with the Hubert's month. As we would begin packing up to go back home, I would anxiously anticipate the arrival of my favorite person in the whole wide world. Minutes seemed like hours and hours seemed like days. My mother would start the process of cleaning about a week before her sister's arrival, tasking me and my little brother, Peter, with simple chores. But my eyes and ears were on the living room picture window facing the long driveway, watching for the yellow Lincoln carrying the precious cargo—God's life-long gift. Finally she would arrive, tan and thin and dressed in pigtails and glasses, her embroidered shorts showing off her long legs (she was so creative). I used to wish God could have made my hair blonde instead of curly and red. But none of that mattered when Grace arrived. Once a year I was transported into a life that did not resemble my life at all. My cousin was the one person in the whole world who saw me for who I was and loved me just as I am. God's love for me shone brightly through her, and I wanted to be just like her.

I loved everything about the Huberts. Grace's father was an executive in education and the funniest adult I knew. He teased me in a sweet, loving way like no other adult ever did. The Huberts were always laughing and teasing, talking about parties and traveling and sports—oh, how they loved baseball, and most of all, hockey! My Uncle Jim had been a goalie for Boston University and was a relief goalie for the Boston Bruins in the 50s. Grace's brothers played high school hockey, and her older sister, Virginia, played on Colby's first college girls' hockey team, inspired by the awe of her father.

There's something special that fills a house with inescapable memories, and that happened when we would all sit around the dining room table. Our dining porch was added on to the original home. We used the original window to pass the food from the kitchen to the dining room, and the original step down from the kitchen to the dining porch from the side door. The porch faced west, so we had the most amazing sunsets over our lake. At the end of the day, the lake was smooth like a glass mirror, reflecting the spectacular sky. As my father was raised in the lumber business, he was a talented furniture maker. He made the extra-long dining room table that could seat fourteen, along with chairs. We would tell stories, tease each other, and play Black Jack for pennies with Grandpa. Oh, how I wished my life could be like this all the time! Laughter filled the air, and I loved the feeling of being included and surrounded by people who were educated, well dressed, witty and fun. The noise felt like a warm hug.

I didn't want anyone to get in between my cousin and me or take the limelight away from me with the rest of the Huberts, which meant I had to get rid of my pesky little brother. I wish I hadn't been so selfish and desperate for attention that I would treat my little brother the same way those children on the street treated me: cruel. It would be one of those regrets of a lifetime later in life, and a life lesson I learned way too late.

Chapter 4

HOME LIFE

In first grade, I attended St. Francis de Sales as my mother was the Physical Education teacher there. At the entrance, you passed through two huge, gold-framed doors with ornate wrought iron protecting the glass. Marble floors led straight down the hall to the classrooms on the first floor. First grade was to the right and second grade to the left. You could always tell the older nuns because their all-black habits went all the way down their back. They had their rosary beads around their waist and looked, well, a little scary. But they were very nice to my brother and me. As I reflect back on those years, I feel as though the nuns were my angels around me in elementary school. They would feed us soup when we had to wait for my mother, and on one trip I took to visit my cousin, Sister Elizabeth Ann was on the bus and offered to sit with me on the ride. When my Grandmother Dick died, I remember Sister Margaret being so kind to me on the playground. They were earthly angels who were there when I needed one.

Life was simple for my brother and me. We were protected from the things that need not concern children, and for that I am truly grateful. But life happens. We lost my father's mother and witnessed the sadness that comes from grief from my grandfather. I can remember him sharing with my dad how she didn't want to live anymore, and he broke down in tears. It was so hard to see that as a young girl. A year later, my mother lost her mother. They were very close, so if was difficult for her. Then on top of all the grief, my dad lost his job as the regional manager for WholeSale Service, a lumber supplier. There was a lot of emotion going on in our family, but no one spoke of it.

Treat. That's what my parents called their time to unwind. It was at six o'clock while they watched the news in the "TV room." Local news first, and then Walter Cronkite. When I heard the news come on the TV, I could almost smell the gin, the Martini and the Manhattan (at least an eight-ounce bomb). My parents would have two of them before dinner. Then the question would come to mind: what would the night be like? Happy and lighthearted? Angry and antagonistic? Emotional? The personality changes that alcohol brought were difficult to navigate. My parents were good people; they certainly were responsible and took good care of their children, but the effect of their drinking had an effect on me.

I was a lighthearted little girl who just wanted to be happy. I was chatty and filled with excitement for life and would get overwhelmed with "awe" when I saw the first snow or heard a song on the radio that I loved. My eyes would well up with joy witnessing the glory of God—just a happy spirit. I didn't like the personality changes alcohol caused in my parents. When we sat down for dinner, I did what I had to do to keep the mood light. I would redirect my father from my brothers by talking about something that would hopefully take him off the topic of the Vietnam War, long hair, rock and roll, friends who weren't "acceptable," or whether or not my mother's dinner had been overcooked. It was a land mine! I was in constant search for the happiness I saw at my friend's house, an easier, lighthearted energy. I used to question my older brothers: why don't we ever laugh? There's no laughter in the house. The weight of my parents' disappointment in life was palpable. I always wanted to be somewhere else. The boys didn't know what I was talking about because, at that point, they were mischievous teenagers who focused on beer and girls. They really didn't care whether their little sister was happy or not. They just didn't want to be inconvenienced, and I was an inconvenience, and a noisy one at that.

One thing that always made me happy was singing. I secretly wanted to be a singer, but my family did not really think it was ever going to be a reality. And then there was getting "thrown out of piano lessons." I was not to be thwarted, despite the constant, "Be quiet! Make her stop singing, Mom!" Nothing could deter me. I would go to our cellar where we had a record player and sing and sing and sing. My parents had albums like Nat King Cole's *Greatest Hits* released in 1968. Oh, how I would belt out "Walking My Baby Back Home." This awkward, freckle-faced redhead with her imaginary microphone, singing and dancing to Nat King Cole, envisioning and praying that someone would "discover her" in her basement. I also loved Bette Midler's 1972 hit "Do you want to Dance?" It described my sweet, innocent, romantic feelings, and I would play it over and over and over again on my little 45 record player, dancing and singing in my bedroom. I acted as if I was auditioning for Davy Jones of The Monkeys or David Cassidy of the Partridge Family, so sure they would discover me in my bedroom.

It filled me with such hope and dreams. I always felt I was destined for greatness. (Wow, what an ego for such a young spirit!) I desperately wanted to be acknowledged, maybe because I didn't feel like I was special in my family. It's also possible that the acknowledgement I did receive was never enough because of my selfish desire to be the center of attention. I would literally suck the life out of the room! Any way you look at it, God blessed me with a spirit that was not going to go quietly into the abyss. I would dance, sing, and laugh, always searching for the thing that was going to give me the feeling I was looking for. Money was tight, and I was always embarrassed for not having the nice clothes or saddle shoes that had leather soles, not rubber. Combine that with self-centered fear. I appeared to be happy, but when I was around other people, I was so uncomfortable with my insides and outsides.

The summers we would spend on the lake were magical! The water was crystal clear, and when we went out to open the lake house Memorial Day weekend in Upstate New York, the air was so crisp and leaves covered the ground.

The lilac trees were in full bloom, even though spring was on its way out and summer on its way in. When we turned in the driveway and heard the gravel under our tires, we knew fun would be had, although we would work hard first. The boys would rake the leaves, and I would help my mother put the porch furniture back on the front porch, vacuum, mop the floors, clean the windows on the porch—so many windows! We cleaned them with newspaper, vinegar, and water. It was the key to streak-less windows for the spectacular sunsets enjoyed out of the dining room.

The lake was like glass, and at the end of the day, the setting sun reflected on the lake was like a mirror to God's glory. It was His canvas. The lake was spring-fed and would freeze in the winter but would be melted by May. After a long day of cleaning and chores, my brother and I would get to take a break and jump off the dock into the water. You couldn't walk in as it was too cold; you had to jump—SPLASH—gasping for breath. Your body hit that freezing cold water, and it would take your breath away! LET'S DO IT AGAIN! We loved the excitement and had so much fun in and out of the water. Up the ladder on the dock, run, and in again. Glass Lake was magical. We couldn't wait until July when we would get to stay the month.

My grandfather built the lake house in the 1930s and had close friends who summered out there. My grandparents were "well-to-do" in the Albany area. He was a successful dentist on State Street, just down the street from the capital of New York, and my grandmother was a successful antique dealer. Her shop was in the bottom of their brownstone, my grandfather's dentist office was on the first floor, and their living space was on the floor above. They were high society in New York's capital in their day. They loved the convenience of driving out to their "piece of heaven" whenever they wished.

Next door to our lake house was Tiftt Beach, named after my grandparents' family friends. The Tiftt's had a public beach, and we had access from our property to go back and forth any time we wanted. We would climb down through the fence of trees that were put up to keep our privacy, but there was an opening for our families to step down into the picnic area, then on to the beach for days, weeks, and years of fun. Tiftt Beach was always a place that exemplified what I was searching for in my life. It was always exciting and a source of new friends. The laughter, shrills, cries, water splashing, burgers and hot dogs cooking on the grill, and chocolate chip ice cream cones. Grandma would always sneak us some money for an ice cream. My grandmother was a mystery to me. She smelled heavenly and dressed to the "nines." She was sophisticated and well-cultured, with no tolerance for disobedience, and she was beautiful.

I loved going to the beach early with all the other children for swim lessons, and I would try to make new friends. It's funny that as I look back, I can still feel that awkward feeling of having to talk with someone new. Would they be nice or would they call me a name? I was filled with that self-centered fear, never thinking that maybe others had their own insecurities. It was always "because I have red hair" that I thought people didn't like me. But if they engaged, I was their best friend. There was a wonderful instructor who was very kind and good looking. Ohhh, I had a crush on Lifeguard Bill. Once I told him I liked him, and he was very sweet with my tender heart. He said, "One day I'll be in my twenties and you'll be in your late teens, and I'll wish that you still felt for me then as you do now!" I hugged him and ran home and cried. Why did life have to be so cruel!

But I am so grateful to God to have grown up with a lake house!

Chapter 5

THE EARLY YEARS

Throughout elementary school, it was a life of nothing extraordinary; day-in and day-out, it was just the same thing: school, playing with my friends, and my attempts at piano lessons. One day after my lesson, my teacher, Sister Elizabeth Ann, told me to tell my mother to come see her when she had a chance. I bounded down the stairs to the balcony overlooking the gym in my little brown and tan checked uniform, red curls bouncing. I yelled down to my mother teaching a Phys. Ed. class.

"Mom, Sister Elizabeth Ann wants to talk with you when you have time."

What she eventually told my mother was to save her money! Piano lessons were not for me. As much as that is a cute, adorable story, it was one of the failures I felt shame about. I struggled with practice. The only time I would sit down to the piano was when my parents were having "treat." They were enjoying their two Martinis and Manhattans with cheese and crackers. They did not want to have me work through "Mary Had a Little Lamb" while they were trying to unwind.

There was so much going on in the world at that time. My brothers were teenagers and rebelling, each in their own way, and the day-in, day-out life was stressful. I can remember always doing the dishes and being grateful for the job as it got me away from the tension, and on a good night, I would get praised for it. My parents did the best they could at handling their own fears of the reality and struggles of life; however, they just weren't present. I guess that's the best way to explain it. There was never the ask about homework, help with piano, encouragement of sports; as long as things didn't interfere with their life, it was all good. They were exhausted just dealing with work and school and driving the boys here and there. I am grateful for all they did.

The times of sweet enjoyment came at the holidays. My mother was a traditionalist, and we had fun helping with the cooking and baking. We would go see the lights at Christmas time, and we were so excited to watch Santa come around on the fire truck. At Easter we had the Easter Bunny, coloring eggs, beautiful baskets every year and getting dressed up with a hat and patent leather shoes. Oh, and the corsage. My dad always got me and my mother a corsage for church. On Valentine's Day, my dad would always bring us a heart-shaped box of chocolate, and on St. Patrick's Day, we had corned beef and cabbage and green beer. There were sparklers at the Fourth of July and toasting marshmallows at the fire. My parents worked hard to give us those special moments; they both worked, and yet they still found the time to make the holidays special.

I remember the outings to the farm where my father grew up. My grandmother, Nana, was an Irish spitfire, though I didn't really know her.

Pappy was my grandfather. He was Swedish and had a successful lumber yard in the town where they lived. Neither were touchy-feely people, so they were not able to engage with little ones. My parents used to do more family outings with friends, bake special treats, and go on picnics when my older brothers were younger, but seven years later when I and my younger brother came along, they were tired and overwhelmed.

Through our formative years, we first lost my mother's mother to a stroke, then my father's mother a year later, also to a stroke. Back-to-back loss was hard on my mother. They left a huge hole in her life. I can remember waking up one day in second grade, bounding out of bed and scurrying out of my pretty, pink room with pink flowered curtains and a pink wool (so itchy) blanket, and into the dining room. I knew my mother was up because of the smell of freshly-perked coffee and toasted bread. Every morning, that's how she started her day, enjoying the quiet before we all emerged. This day was different. Mom was sitting in the chair next to the island that separated the dining room from the kitchen, coffee and toast getting cold, and she was just crying. As I went to hug her, she said "You're the only friend I have left." It was a moment that knitted a sense of responsibility for my mother's happiness in me, and I was determined, in my sweet eight-year-old self, to never let her cry like that again. Unfortunately, through my "windy, broken road," I am sure that I was the cause of many tears that flowed much heavier than those of the grief of losing her mother.

My growing up years were filled with me trying to find ways to feel comfortable in my own skin. We couldn't afford to have the best of anything, as money was tight. It didn't matter much when I was at St. Francis de Sales, as we had a uniform, and it was the innocent elementary years. The only thing I got in trouble for was talking in class. It was too much to ask for me not to talk at all in class. How was I going to make friends if I couldn't chat?

" Kathleen Mary! Out in the hall."

I knew then that I wouldn't be able to hide my troublemaking from my mother. Thank goodness it was only Mother Superior who would see me, but I knew she would tell my mother. The worst part of me getting in trouble was always the disappointment I would be to her. I had vowed to protect her from any pain, and there I was, embarrassing her at the school where she taught.

Later, my mother got a job in the Utica Public School System, which meant we switched to public school. I was excited to ride the bus and meet new friends. I naively thought my neighborhood "friends" who picked on me as a little one would embrace me as a transfer student. Friendships were already established when I came into the new school, but there were some who were kind and made the effort to get to know me. Carole Z. and Karen B. became my besties. Fifth grade was a whole new experience. I needed school clothes because there were no uniforms, and that was where the self-centered fear raised its ugly head! I was so uncomfortable with how I looked and didn't think I looked like the popular kids. I was filled with the fear they wouldn't like me. My shoes had rubber soles instead of leather, and my jeans were from Kmart and not a department store. I felt like I wasn't like the rest of the pretty girls. I didn't have the perfect figure; I was pear-shaped like my mother and grandmother, which was not an attractive feature in those days. I didn't feel funny enough or smart enough. Then there was the hair—oh, how I hated my red hair. I had no idea how to coif my locks, so it was thick and wavy and didn't look like my other friends. I was always so self-conscious that I didn't know how I could make people like me.

Then there was my little brother Peter, who was heavy because he was born prematurely and had some sort of problem with weight. It wasn't because of bad diet; it was just a physiological thing. The rule was I could make fun of him but no one else could. If I thought making fun of him would get me attention, I am truly ashamed to say, I did. However, if one of the children on the bus said anything about him, I would go up to them and give them a piece of my mind. It is sad to think of that double standard. My need to look good at any cost, including my brother's feelings, led to just plain cruel behavior. It's funny how we can rationalize and justify ourselves, but the truth of the matter was, I was desperate to be accepted. Peter was my best friend and constant companion, and I was his worst nightmare.

Chapter 6

NO, IT WASN'T A DREAM

My age of innocence ended during the summer between sixth and seventh grade in 1974. I would be going to a different school for seventh grade, and I felt so grown up. The summers at Glass Lake now had become boring. I just needed something to make me feel better.

My innocence ended with the "heist." There was a lot of planning and timing that went into procuring the magic elixir. We had to be on constant watch for the perfect moment when the adults weren't around and everyone was distracted. I grabbed a mason jar and just started opening bottles and pouring, careful not to take too much out of any one bottle. My heart was racing. I could smell the gin used to make Martinis, the rye for Manhattans, and the vermouth (red and white) to whisper over the cocktails. SLAM! The cabinet was closed, and I was out of the kitchen. I hid the jar in the back bedroom my cousin and I stayed in. No one would look there.

Then came the painful wait. When night fell, my cousin and I disappeared into the back bedroom of the lake house, wondering if we would be missed. We could hear the chatter and laughter from the adults, ice tinkling in the summer drink of choice—Whiskey Sours—and we could smell the cigarette smoke thick in the air as everyone smoked more with their cocktails.

We knew now was the time to grab the concoction, sneak out the window, and head down to the beach. The moonlight danced on ripples in the water from jumping fish and reflected bright white on the the lake. It was quiet by the water; the light from the pinball machine at the Beach Grill felt like a floodlight as we snuck away so the adults couldn't see us from the porch. I felt energized from the adrenaline running through my veins; the anticipation was palpable. I couldn't wait to open the jar. Finally, we were alone. The top made a suction sound as it twisted open, and the liquor smell was strong as it breathed. It was the scent of Dad's Martinis and Mother's Manhattans. I couldn't wait for my turn to have a "treat." Then the long-awaited sip. It burned as it went down, but a warmth rose inside my twelve-year-old self. I couldn't wait for the next swig. This time the burn was a little less. My shoulders dropped, and a relaxed feeling overwhelmed me with a peace and joy I'd never felt before. There was a sense of relief.

Relief. Relief from what? I was twelve!

That relief was from feeling different, for constantly trying to fit in, from self-centered fear, from constantly trying to get people to acknowledge my existence, even though I demanded all the attention at all times. It was relief from the home I lived in that felt like a gray cloud was always hovering, relief from the financial strain of my middle-class parents trying to raise five children when Dad was out of work and had to settle for being a hardware store manager at Kmart after being a regional sales manager for a lumber company. Relief from my mother, who wanted so much more out of life, who was ahead of her time and wanted her husband to have an adventure with her, something he was not interested in joining her at all. Or the grief that wasn't discussed from my mother who lost her mother and my father who lost his mother. Relief from the stress and anger of three teenage boys and the Vietnam War, the tense arguments that took place every night at the dinner table where all I could do was remove myself by doing the dishes.

I'm so thankful there was no abuse, and I know my parents did the best they knew how. They were just overwhelmed and didn't have a community of people who could help them turn to a relationship with God. God is the one who brings real peace and joy even amidst the trials of life—not the false sense I received from the alcohol. I feel like the Protestants were much better at community than the Catholics. Catholic growing up meant anxiety, guilt, and frustration getting to church, then an hour of gymnastics during the service, the sermon that was the priest's interpretation of today's issues, and the sermon that always felt like we were being "scolded" for living. The pièce de résistance at church was going from "peace be with you" to "get out of my way" as everyone was fighting to get out of the parking lot the fastest. Such a powerful message! These were the things that I needed relief from.

In addition to that, I was born with the disease. When that alcohol hit that sweet, little twelve-year-old brain, it was all I could do to not jump up and down for joy. I felt I'd found the elixir that made everything fun and happy; all I'd ever wanted was just a little laughter and lightheartedness. As we emptied the jar and the alcohol rose to my young brain, I thought, "This is how I want to feel ALL the time." I made a vow that I would do whatever it took to feel that way—and I lived up to that vow.

The funny thing about alcoholism is that we think it shows up when we are at a point in our lives where we are drinking heavily and laden with troubles, but the disease starts when we first put alcohol into our system and an allergic reaction takes place. My body demanded more. Yes, there was a progression, and in my case, there certainly was no "shut off." But thinking back, it is amazing to think that as an innocent twelve-year-old, I poured that poison into my body and didn't get terribly sick. It didn't bother me to feel out of control. No, I just couldn't wait to do it again. Alcoholics are funny that way. Even if you do get sick or get into terrible trouble because of alcohol, there is never the thought, "Gee, I probably shouldn't keep drinking," or "I'm never going to do that again." The baffling thing is, even if they have that thought, they rationalize and justify it so that the next time alcohol is presented, they forget all the problems, pain, and trouble that it caused the last time they drank. They pick up a drink again, and the cycle continues, over and over again. That is what I did! That is a definition of insanity: to do the same thing over and over again, expecting a different result. The disease takes away the best parts of you. It takes away the loyalty to your friends or putting their needs and safety first. You only do whatever you can do to drink the way you want to. This behavior hurts people who love you! I would say, "I'm sorry," over and over and over again until it became white noise.

I entered seventh grade with a false sense of confidence and false maturity due to my newfound "friend." God had blessed me with my best friends, Karen and Carol, and we would do everything together. School was so exciting as we went up to Parkway School, our entry into middle school. This school had all the elementary schools in the district come together. We changed classrooms, had lockers, and had a whole new set of friends. I felt like I stepped into adulthood. The reality was, I hadn't even stepped into my teen years. The groups split off into their comfort zones: basketball players, football players, cheerleaders, science club. I had a crush on a basketball player—the quiet, tall, dark and handsome young man type. We would hold hands in the hall and meet at parties; the keg parties behind the tracks were where we went as teenagers. We would make our way through neighborhoods into fields. I guess I told my parents it was a bonfire? We thought we were acting like adults even though we were children.

It was the school dance, and my best friend and I were so excited. We got dressed up, wore make-up, put on a pretty outfit, and went to the dance. My friend and I walked into the dance, but almost immediately snuck out behind the school to drink. I remember the thrill when we arrived outside on the field. We had a new friend in school who had an older brother who bought us liquor—Red Lady 21 wine and blackberry brandy. What a combination! It left me rolling around in the grass, abandoning my sweet friend. That was what alcohol did for me. I dragged my friend Karen along to get into trouble. That was the nature of our friendship. We had lots of laughs along the way, for sure, but alcohol was making my decisions for me, and I wasn't concerned about anyone else. I was pursuing that elusive feeling that I craved. Oh, the lies of the enemy. "This will be fun. They are going to love you. You'll finally fit in. The guys will see you as cool and attractive." But the reality of alcohol took me to incomprehensible demoralization, shame, humiliation, dishonesty and guilt.

"KATHY QUINN! GET IN THIS SCHOOL RIGHT NOW!"

It was Mr. Putrello, a robust, heavy, Italian man. He and Mr. Johnson (oh, I had such a crush on him, my science teacher) were the chaperones at the dance. Mr. Putrello asked who gave us the alcohol, and I told him I didn't know. My friend kicked me in the behind. "Kathy, tell him or I am."

"We are not going to be tattletales," I said. Karen was always my window into doing the "right" thing, but I always chose the rebellious approach.

Mr. Putrello walked us through the crowd of

students gathered to see what was going on outside. You could hear the whispers from the students, "What were they doing? Is that Kathy Quist? Is she drunk? Were they drinking on the football field?"

I don't know whether the other guys who were with us got in trouble. I think they ran off. I was brought into the principal's office, and Karen was in with the vice principal. After some questioning, I had to call my parents, and the principal told my dad I got caught drinking at the school dance. The wait for my father to arrive felt like forever. The brown Buick pulled up in front of the junior high, and my dad came in and thanked the principal.

I can remember the feeling of remorse covering me, and there was nothing I could say; my behavior said it all. I just kept my head down, tears of embarrassment, shame and grief enveloping me at the reality of the disappointment I brought to my father, and if I'm honest, the regret I had that I got caught. The ride home was silent; it felt like a heavy blanket of shame and disappointment, with just the sound of the motor and the brakes when slowing to stop. I looked out the window and knew the "conversation" would be following in the morning. Sadly, as I reflect back on this memory, I see how quickly the devil stole my identity of the sweet girl who wanted to have fun and cared about bringing love, joy and protection to her loved ones through her love of Jesus. Not once did I think about how Karen felt, or what was happening at home for her, or how I should have never brought her out to that dark football field with strangers and a poison to be ingested that would guarantee pain for each of us, our parents, or the extra work and disappointment of the teachers. I only thought of the relief and how it made me feel. Honestly, if asked at that time if I would do it again, I would sadly say yes!

I knew I had to go upstairs to face my parents. I so wished I hadn't gotten caught. What would I do about school? What would I say to my teachers, principal, friends? Everyone would be talking about what happened the night of our first school dance. I'll deal with that later! Upstairs I went. Obviously, after such shameful actions, I knew I was going to have consequences, and of course I did.

"YOU'RE GROUNDED!"

Those words were repeated quite a bit in my teen years. My parents' disappointment was palpable. They only wanted me to have a good life filled with love and laughter. My mother prayed that I would "find my way." The enemy told me I had found my way. I did not take the path that led to a strong relationship with God; I took the path that stepped into the Dark Forest. Trying to navigate an adult life with the emotional maturity of a twelve-year-old led to living a life in the shadows.

"The people who walked in darkness
have seen a great light; those who
dwelt in a land of deep darkness, on
them has light shined."
Isaiah 9:2

It took a long time for the light to shine; I just kept walking deeper and deeper into an alcoholic abyss. The devil had already placed a stronghold on my young life. He became my compass, with alcohol greasing the path for me to slide down a rapid slope leading me into the Dark Forest. What should have been a sweet, innocent experience of my first school dance ended up being a snapshot of what my life was going to be like as I entered the lifestyle of drinking, followed shortly along with drugs. Imagine using the tools of a child and navigating the adult world of drinking and drugging, walking into the trap the enemy set so I would not live out the plans God had for my life and His Kingdom. But God always takes care of His children, even when we don't know we need protection.

> *"Behold I send an angel before you to*
> *guard you on the way and to bring*
> *you to the place that I have prepared."*
> Exodus 23:20

I remember praying that night, "Please, please, please, Lord, make it a dream." This prayer became my constant prayer as alcohol took a leading role in my young life. It was no dream. As the years went on, I would lie in bed thinking about what had gone on the night before. I would get that pit in my stomach, the one you get when you know you were out of alignment with God. I couldn't feel Him then. I would say, "I'm sorry," but only to get my life turned around enough so I could do what I wanted again. My prayers to Him at this stage were only 911 prayers. I made a mess of life, and I just wanted the mess to go away. The overwhelming thought of my shameful behavior was too much for me to process. My coping tool was to push those feelings down and tell myself to get it together. That was my mind's pep talk. That sweet, young girl was nowhere to be seen. The wild child had taken over, and she was going to drive the bus. She found the relief in alcohol, and nothing was going to get in the way of it or take it away. Whatever problem was occurring as a result was just a mess that could get cleaned up and eventually forgotten.

> *"Be sober minded; be watchful.*
> *Your adversary the devil prowls*
> *around like a roaring lion, seeking*
> *someone to devour."*
> 1 Peter 5:8

As the time went on, and I was no longer grounded, I continued to go to parties on the tracks and would spend time visiting my boyfriend, Jack Bella. These times together always centered around alcohol. There was a corner bar we went to; even at such a young age, we were allowed in. Beers were twenty-five cents, and there was a pool table and foosball, a child's playground with adult beverages. I liked having a boyfriend and tried to make Jack be who I needed him to be. We broke up because he was controlling. He told me I couldn't visit my cousin, and I thought, "This isn't working for me."

In high school, my choices for nice young men included the principal's son, Joe, who wasn't such a great choice as he was a year younger, and I was definitely not spending time in a healthy way. We went to the Winter Ball. My friend Carol's boyfriend was also a year younger, so we all hung out together. My friend Karen started dating Jimmy in ninth grade, and he was and still is the love of her life. They were so cute and fun, and she knew he was the one!

As we progressed in school, my disease progressed. Pot became a big part of my day-in, day-out life. High school was nothing but a party. All the things I should have been doing as a student and a girl developing into a young woman were thwarted because my only focus was alcohol, parties, and how I was going to be perceived by my peers.

Chapter 7

FIRST LOVE, THE DEVIL'S TRAP

KABOOM! The fireworks exploded over the lake in Old Forge, New York, and they weren't half as exciting as the ones that were exploding inside my body!

The summer of my junior year, I met the "one"—Tommy O'Sullivan. That Fourth of July I had gone up to Old Forge with a group of friends. I had never done that before because I was usually at Glass Lake with my family, but I had my first job, so my parents allowed me to stay home from the lake house to work. This job paid money, unlike my volunteer job as a candy-striper. I sold Karmel Korn, and oh how yummy it was! Warm and gooey just out of the copper kettle. This was my summer to do all the things I always wanted to do without my parents.

We drank beer the whole way to Old Forge, and then at the park the real party began! There were all sorts of groups of people there enjoying the festivities. I met a group of friends I was immediately attracted to, primarily because of the tall, dark-haired, blue-eyed young man. It was magic when our eyes connected. I say magic because I don't believe God was divinely orchestrating this union; chemistry, beer, and marijuana was more the influence. I was smitten, to say the least. He was older, had graduated two years before me, worked at Baker's Flowers, and he had a group of friends I instantly loved. They were fun and funny and had a bond I admired. I felt like I had found the love of my life. He asked for my number, and I invited him and his friends to a party I was having. I prayed he would call, and he did! When I picked him up from work, he had a bouquet of roses for me. When I met his family, they were a dream-come-true Irish family that was everything I always wanted. I thought it was meant to be.

Tommy invited me to the home of his friends Terry and Paula Love. They were a wonderful couple, jovial, inclusive, fun; there was also the added benefit of being marijuana farmers. Paula worked with Tommy at a flower shop distributor and was gifted with plants, like a little garden fairy. Terry and Paula grew pot in the back fields, and it was always a party at the Love's farm. That night with Tommy was magical. All their friends came up, and we drank, smoked pot, and told stories. I felt like I had found the perfect life, as only a sixteen-year-old would think. A wonderful group of people, everyone loved to party the way I did, all the laughter and music. They loved the band Genesis like I did, and we listened until the wee hours. I knew what my path was; I was going to marry this man. I had saved myself for the perfect guy, and he was it. We were together whenever we weren't working.

I was ready for the party at my house: keg, check; chips, check; solo cups, check. IT IS ON!! The party day was here, and I prayed all my new friends would come, especially Tommy. I knew all my high school friends would come. The anxiety of messing up my parents' furniture, concern about spillage, thinking maybe I shouldn't have done this—nooooo!!! I couldn't go down that path. Everything was going to be fine. I told myself not to listen to the voice within, to get my head right! The party will be great, and everyone will have a ball!

The only way I knew how to quiet the Lord's voice that was directing me to the path of righteousness was to give myself a pep talk and drink. Ok, one beer down. Now it was, "Let's get this party started." The music was loud, and the cars kept coming. I really wasn't experienced in throwing a party. I never even thought about my neighbors, parking, the bathroom, the bedrooms. I just drank. The police came and told us to turn down the music, and THEN the call came. My father.

"What the hell is going on there? We are coming to get you, and everyone better be gone!"

Well, that certainly sobered me up! My friends stayed to get the house picked up: plastic cups, cigarettes, my friend Carol taught me how to get water rings off of the furniture with mayonnaise. We were maniacs trying to get the house cleaned up. A couple of my friends took the beer. The impending doom was settling in, and I knew I was going to be in big trouble. I definitely wasn't going to get to stay home and have the summer party I had planned for the rest of the month. I didn't know how I would ever build my trust back with my parents. How could such a wonderful night turn out so badly? Maybe I should have listened to that voice.

It was a very quiet, long ride to Glass Lake. The next day, I was officially grounded. I had already assumed that since I had been removed from all my friends and any summer parties. It took time for my parents to be at all engaged with me. Other than the yes or no's, there wasn't a lot of chitchat or banter. I was so traumatized that I couldn't see my new boyfriend. I wanted to tell my mother all about him, but she was in no mood to hear about me meeting the love of my life—all sixteen years of it.

"IT'S ALL GONE!"

My mother was sheet-white, her ear to the phone. When my dad went home a week after the party, he found our home in shambles. We had been robbed! All their beautiful silver from their wedding, heirlooms passed down, and jewelry from her mother. I was sick. I tried to convince myself that it was unrelated to the party, but I knew it had to be. I just didn't know how.

My parents were devastated. The Sheriff's Department conducted the investigation and found some of the items at pawn shops. The news spread like wildfire through my circle of friends. Tommy's brother Mark said he might know something about it. Mark was the black sheep of the O'Sullivan family and no stranger to the law. He had done a few shady things in his past, and he knew a few shady characters, but he was a good guy with a good heart. He came to me and told me he had heard one of the guys boasting about the big score they made! SCORE! How awful it sounded for supposed friends of mine to be boasting that my parents' robbery was a big SCORE! I was truly in a state of shock from my naiveté. I just couldn't fathom that friendship didn't mean anything and only the money was the motive. The two culprits were George and Roland. My friend George and I had planned the party to make it special for his girlfriend Sally's birthday, and another guy I went to school with and partied with, Roland Short, staked the house out while at the party. When my parents came to get me, they knew the house would have no one home. I bought pot from Roland and had the party with George so he could celebrate his girlfriend. I just couldn't believe it! How could they? I thought they were my friends. We went to the Sheriff's Department and told them what we knew.

It was a crazy time. I was surrounded by signs from God that the path I was on was the wrong path, and yet I was sure all was well. I was sure that God wouldn't give me this feeling of love for this handsome Irishman if he wasn't the one, and I was sure he wouldn't give me this wonderful group of friends who were such a tight-knit group that I wanted to be included in. I was like Jonah in the Bible; I thought I could out-run, out-smart, and hide from God so I could get my way, but God had a storm, actually many storms, ready to convince me otherwise. He sent the school dance incident, He sent the party where I ran into a glass sliding door (miraculously not breaking it), He sent the principal's office and the consequences for skipping school. But I still didn't see it.

Pastor Greg Laurie in his Crosspoint Devotions says this: "That storm came as a result of Jonah's disobedience. I call it a correcting storm. Correcting storms are what we basically bring upon ourselves by our stupid actions. We do something wrong. It catches up with us. We face the consequences. And then we say, 'Oh, why has this storm come into my life?' It's because of what we did. That's why."

I was an incredibly strong-willed young woman, and I wasn't going to let go of this new life. My new friends escaped the way I wanted to escape. I had made my way into their group, and I wasn't going to let that all go because of the signs that screamed, "Get your life together! It's going to get worse!"

And it did get worse.

Chapter 8

AFTER THE LOVE IS GONE

Tommy left for a job in Idaho, and I was left behind to finish school. It was so scary to think of letting him go. I had a great group of friends, but it still wasn't going to feel the same. We would write, but oh, how I would miss him! We had a sweet, romantic experience while we were dating, but I was saving myself for our wedding night! I was sure he would understand that; what man wouldn't want that? I was so sad, but my friends, the drinking, and getting high, were a constant source of comfort. We wrote letters here and there, and then there was the "one letter" I had waited so long for, the one I so wanted that said he really thought we had something "incredibly special," and he thinks about me "all the time." It was confirmed in my mind that he was in love with me as much as I was in love with him!

As spring began, Tommy would be coming home. He had hurt his back and couldn't work construction any longer. My prayers had been answered! I was so nervous getting ready to see him. I wanted to look perfect and imagined this incredible, romantic reunion, one where he couldn't keep focused on anything other than me. All I could think about and dream about was the night he would come home. When I did see him, it took my breath away. He was happy to see me, but thinking of it now, the anticipation was much more than the reality of the reunion. I felt like there was something I was missing. He seemed a little preoccupied when we all got together. Tommy and I went off to be alone; we petted for awhile, and then he said he had a headache. I didn't hear from him the next day, or the day after, and then the call came. He said he was sorry, but he didn't want to go out anymore. He had grown out of our relationship.

How could this be? I was devastated! How could he not feel the same way I did? I knew it was because I didn't go "all the way" with him. He wanted sex, and I was too naive to understand what was happening.

His friends were wonderful, but they were also loyal to Tommy. I wasn't going to give him up without a fight. So I did what every broken-hearted girl does—I stalked him. We would all go places, and I would hope to see him at the bar or the party. I would try to find out where he was going and who he was with. If I did see him at the party or a bar, my heart would stop. I would say hello as if I was so cool, but my heart was broken in a million pieces. I was crying all the time. My mother couldn't comfort me; my friends tried to. I went on and on about him and would play music about broken hearts over and over again on my record player. I couldn't get him off my mind.

Time heals all wounds, and eventually my heart began to heal.

Through this time, Tommy's best friend Bob (they called him Sloany) was especially attentive. I didn't realize it at the time, but he had a crush on me. He was sweet, but not what my heart wanted. He listened to me cry for hours about his best friend. Finally he had to say something.

"Why can't you see the guy who is in love with you is right here?" Well, that stopped me in my tracks. I was seventeen and filled with confusion. Bob? Sloany? Well, ok. I loved his boldness. Bob had seen me at my best and at my worst. He liked me for me. I felt I had to move on. Why not with him?

I had no compass to make decisions. I didn't know to take time to discuss the situation with God or wise women. I never stopped to ask my Heavenly Father for comfort or confirmation that I was doing the right thing. I n ever took the opportunity to spend time developing my relationship with the Lord or allow Jesus to be my Comforter or my guide about the next decision I was about to make. I just said yes, and Bob and I became an item. I had worn myself out with grief. Having Bob's attention made me feel special. These are the ways that the enemy steals, kills, and destroys. It's never through the obvious attack; it's subtle. When I was desperate to feel differently, the enemy always provided me with an immediate solution. A drink, a drug, a man, anything to make me feel different than how I felt. The enemy was not going to let me find the comfort from "the Comforter," he wasn't going to allow me to find healing through God's Word. No, no, no. Just catapult me into another situation with a different way to think and the path of disease was on.

Bob lived on the same street as Tommy, but his family wasn't like Tommy's family. Tommy had a lovely home with a mom who was fit and energetic. They had a pool and a lot of joking in the house. Tommy showed great affection for his mother and respect for his dad. Bob's home did not have the same happy vibe. Bob and I had the same feelings about our families—we wished they were different. He wanted so much more, just as I did. And just like that, we were an item.

Bob was my senior year relationship. We went to all the parties, all my formal dances. We were inseparable. I still secretly had feelings for Tommy, but Bob was a great guy, and I was "in love" with him. We would go to parties, go camping, and hang out with Terry and Paula up on the farm. He was a gentleman in the sense of his kindness; he held the door for me and opened my car door. He worked at a gas station and at his father's company. I thought all was well as I lived a very adult life with the emotional maturity of a twelve-year-old. I had no idea that the decisions I was about to make would affect me for a lifetime!

Bob loved me for who I was and was patient with me. Then one day, we were on my parents' couch. No one was home nor would be for the afternoon. We were kissing, and I was thinking, "Should I? I really think I love him, and I don't want to lose him." Then it was all over. I lost my virginity. I thought I would feel fireworks. I thought I was going to feel more like a woman. I thought I would feel more love. But really the only thing it left me feeling was a pit in my stomach, the feeling I had when I did something wrong, and I couldn't change it. I was a myriad of emotions, none of which were happy and glowing and floating on air, which is what I assumed I would feel. These feelings were more of shame, and thoughts of, "I had better get my head wrapped around this or the emotions will be taking me to a very dark place." It was very much like the feeling when I woke up and couldn't remember what I did the night before, like the school dance when all I wanted to do was pretend that it never happened. The feeling of impending doom.

Doom is a word for death, and that was the reason for that feeling. It was death: the death of my purity, the death of holding something of value for myself to be used for God's partner. The impending part was because I was playing with a recipe that is so miraculous; it brings life into the world, and I was not ready for that. I wanted to feel special, but all I felt was alone, ashamed, and that I had made another decision I couldn't change. I couldn't pretend that it didn't happen. It did—my virginity was GONE, and I would never be the same. I knew it, and God knew it. I never took this life-changing experience to God or even thought to have a discussion with Him about what it would look like if I went down that path. Rules are not to control you, they are to protect you, and this command from our Father was for the protection of a gift that was only to be opened by the one whom the Lord brought to me.

Sex changes everything in relationships! It doesn't matter what approach you take to it—"I love him," or, "I can have recreational sex." There is a bond that forms when you become one with someone. It is meant to be a bond that is for your forever someone. God created us to fit together with our lifetime love. At seventeen, I didn't know what I wanted. My whole life was before me. Bob was wonderful, but I did not have the tools to discern if this was a lifetime love or just someone to spend time with. I believed the lie that the enemy wanted me to—"It's not a big deal; you can have it all now. This will make your life wonderful." That lie tore into my soul and defined me moving forward. Outwardly I clung to the lie, but I believed in the recesses of my mind that I was dirty and therefore had no value in anyone's eyes and certainly not God's eyes. The enemy wants us to feel a part of the darkness and to live in secrets, shadows—hiding and lying—presenting one way to our parents and completely another with our friends. I learned at an early age how to live a double life. The enemy's goal is to STEAL, KILL and DESTROY, and he succeeded in my life with that one act.

When I couldn't accept accountability for my actions, I would rationalize and justify my behavior. I would push the feelings of shame, remorse, and self-hate down and step out in the light, acting as if nothing "life-altering" had just happened. I look back to that young girl, and my heart breaks for her. She kept herself protected by separating herself from her true feelings, and that fueled her need for more drugs and alcohol to get that feeling of wholeness she felt that night when she first had that alcohol.

Chapter 9

THE UNSPOKEN

Please, God, noooo!

I had missed my period. Oh, well, maybe it was just a fluke. Further into the second month, I started to get nervous. Could it be? NO, NO, NO, it couldn't be. I can't tell my parents; this will destroy them. I can't tell my friends. I have so many plans for my future! I was destined for great things! I didn't know what those great things were, but I was going after the world with all the gusto I could muster. I was NOT staying in Utica, New York, and raising a baby! What can I do? This can't be happening!

I went to Planned Parenthood and had an exam. I was too naive at this point to realize I willingly walked into a building that had death draped all around it. All I wanted was to get out of trouble. It was so . . . . clinical. The nurses were kind as they were fully aware what horror lay before me. I remember meeting with a counselor, and she asked if I was sure this was "MY CHOICE." I answered, "Yes," but the thought, "There is another way," was almost audible.

I had no relationship with Jesus, just a faith based on the feelings of peace and love that I received whenever I was in church. My mother taught me my prayers as a girl, and I truly am grateful for them because they were a constant source of comfort in the years that followed. I was raised Catholic, and it was all about the religion and sacraments, but the emphasis was not on a personal relationship with Jesus or His Word. At least, that is not what I understood. I don't remember ever hearing that you can hear the Holy Spirit almost audibly. I did that day when I heard the words, "There's another way." I wanted to do the right thing. I thought about adoption. NO, NO. I'm here already. My fear took over! The clinic was so cold and sterile, chilling really, and everyone had a somber look. I couldn't focus on anything other than myself and my situation. I felt so alone and filled with fear.

My name was called, and my heart sank. Please, God, please, make this be a bad dream. I thought about having the baby and giving it up for adoption, but nine months of pregnancy and having to tell my parents was too much to think about. All I could think was, "Oh, what have I done?"

I had a friend at school who was a strong woman and made the choice to have her baby. I so admire her courage and clarity. She endured being ridiculed at school. I know because I was one of the "friends" who judged her. Today she is one of my heroes. I did not know how to stand in character like my friend Milly. I was selfish and grandiose as I chose to have "my way" all the time. I chose the way that would allow me to continue on with "my plans" for my life. I was not taught the promises of the Lord through His beautiful Word. If I'm honest, I don't know whether I would have chosen to believe His promises at that point in my life. But what would have happened if I had chosen to listen to what I knew to be right? I will never know until I am home in heaven.

> *"'For I know the plans I have for you,'*
> *declares the Lord, 'plans to prosper*
> *you and not to harm you, plans to*
> *give you hope and a future.'"*
> Jeremiah 29:11

I chose my way instead of praying for direction and courage in Jesus' name. I rationalized and justified my decision in MY name, but the pit in my stomach ate away at my soul. The enemy orchestrates every detail for the sinner to move forward with his own destructive plans. The enemy comes to kill (the baby), steal (your soul for making the decision), and destroy (the light that was in our spirit of innocence).

This decision was not a lie about where I was or my drinking; this was the decision to end a life, and I knew it in the depth of my soul. I felt the chill of death as I went into the exam room. I put on the gown and prepared to be examined. Yes, I was pregnant, around eight to twelve weeks, which felt right. I scheduled the appointment and made the mechanics of the decision operational. I had to get the money, which was $400. That was a lot of money. My friend Chrystal said she would talk with her sister. I am so remorseful that I put her sister into such a terrible position.

Her sister knew me as a young girl, since I've known Chrystal since elementary school. The selfishness that caused me to include these beautiful women into my problem was beyond the scope of friendship. Her sister said she would help me because she had a very good job. So I borrowed the money from her, and I was set for the procedure. I am so ashamed of involving them in my destructive plan.

The root of my self-centeredness was deep, and therefore I chose not to tell Bob because I didn't want to explore any discussion that would oppose my decision. It was such a selfish act, since the baby was just as much his as it was mine, but I surrounded myself with people who supported my decisions. I was determined to continue with my plan for my life, and nothing was going to get in the way. I had hardened my heart, and I had no support to change my hardened heart. I wasn't seeking God's will for me or for His baby He gifted me with. He blessed me with a new life, and I felt it was a death sentence. I in turn passed that death sentence on to my baby.

The Pro-Choice narrative states that your baby is not a life in the womb. They tell you that "they" are not real, that it is "just cells." But if you simply Google the development of a fetus, by eight weeks of pregnancy, a baby has already developed its hands and feet. According to whattoexpect.com, the tiny fingers and toes are forming, and the color of the baby's eyes are developing. Although it would have been too soon to tell if it was a boy or a girl, my baby's genitals were already starting to form.

On the Planned Parenthood website, it says, "People who oppose abortion often call themselves pro-life. However, the only life many of them are concerned with is the life of the fertilized egg, embryo, or fetus. They are much less concerned about the life of women who have unintended pregnancies or the welfare of children after they're born. In fact, many people who call themselves "pro-life" support capital punishment (AKA the death penalty) and oppose child welfare legislation."

It is a caldron of debate that has plagued the 21st century. But we have to remember who we are dealing with; the enemy is a master manipulator. Planned Parenthood covers the truth of what they are doing with the blanket of the lie that those who are pro-life don't care about the child's welfare after being born or they accuse them of supporting capital punishment. They shame a woman's decision to take God's choice and for making the decision for the child's life.

I believe the nurses in Planned Parenthood have to believe the lie that they are somehow "helping" the woman by giving her the "Right to Choose." Otherwise, how could they get up each day knowing what they are doing? Especially since they took the oath of protecting life at any cost. In their code of ethics, "it exemplifies the profession's promise to provide and advocate for safe, quality care for all patients and communities. Upholding their commitment to patients and communities requires significant courage and resilience. It involves the willingness to speak out, whether alone or collectively, to do what is right

for patients and other nurses" (https://
www.nursingworld.org/practice-policy/nursing-
excellence/ethics/code-of-ethics-for-nurses).

The Nurses Code of Ethics ensures the safety of the patient and community in all care delivery. Nurses are responsible for reporting treatment options that are causing significant harm to a patient, which may include suicidal or homicidal ideation. By supporting the rationalization and justification of my decision to abort my baby, they were actually giving the permission to kill. I was stepping into an environment that must be somewhat like hell; it appears to be on the "up and up," but it is all smoke and mirrors.

I don't remember a lot of the details of the morning of the abortion. I couldn't shake the gravity of the day and what I was going to do. I was numb to the mixed bag of emotions, allowing me to move forward with the decision. It was like I was in another world or subconscious (which I know today was the Holy Spirit trying to break through to my soul). As I sat there in the waiting room listening for them to call my name, I looked around at the others. There was a heaviness of deep sadness you could cut with a knife. Somber was the expression on everyone of us. Some eyes were filled with tears or had tear stains on their face. Others just had vacant expressions. We were not capable of feeling the depth of our decision. Some women were with the birth fathers, friends, or parents, and some were alone like me. The common theme was that we all knew, at the depth of our soul, what we were about to do.

"Kathy Quinn."

My heart sank with the sound of my name. Be brave, you can do this. My heart raced faster, and I felt like I was holding my breath. I couldn't breathe. I was mechanical in my response to movement and questions. When I got into the sterile procedure room, I changed and lay down. Everything around me in that room was cold and intimidating. When the nurses came in, they explained the procedure. I said I understood and closed my eyes, as if it would make everything go away. I didn't want to see anything, as if that would make it an illusion. The machine went on and the sound was deafening—the suction and pull on my abdomen was the life getting ripped out of me. I am so very sorry to my baby for that horrific experience.

Now that I am a Christian, I know that Jesus was in the room, not for me, but to escort my sweet baby to heaven. And there our babies wait for us. They have forgiven us. My journey was to seek the forgiveness of Jesus, and through His mercy, find the forgiveness for myself. There were a lot of years before that peace came. I pray you don't have to follow the path of degradation that I did to try to escape the self-hate, remorse, and shame of my decision. If you have followed that same path, know that you are forgiven and loved. Just ask Jesus for the forgiveness you have tried to provide throughout your life yet never could achieve!

At the end of the procedure, I felt empty. Not just physically, but I felt numb to any feeling, like the walking dead. I went home, went to my room, and cried. I tried to sleep it away. I didn't know how I was going to push the experience down. I had already packed my heart with so many shameful and remorseful experiences, but this one was so big. I didn't know if I would be able to move through my life acting like nothing happened to me. Bob did not have a say in this experience. I justified my decision with the pro-choice narrative, "My Body My Choice." I now see how harmful, selfish, and just wrong that was. Bob deserved to have a say, but how could he have a say if he didn't know there was even something to talk about? I was so afraid of being convinced to do something I didn't want to do. It was a terrible thing to do to someone you "love." When I did get up the courage to tell him, h e was wonderful. He was pensive, but he supported my decision. I can't tell you whether he was relieved or not. It wasn't spoken of again.

When I got back to my old self, I felt as though I had been through a tragedy, which in fact I had. But I somehow couldn't bring myself to accept the truth of what I had done. For me to get out of bed and face the world, I had to make peace with myself. Since I knew Jesus was the only peace, and I now felt I couldn't come to Him because I was a filthy rag, I had to create my own false peace. I felt I could NEVER be forgiven for what I had done. I had made my bed, and now I had to lie in it. I had never felt so alone. The only feeling of peace I ever felt was with Him, and now I felt I wasn't worthy to ask for His time or forgiveness. I made the decision that I was going to live a BIG HUGE LIFE and experience everything that this fallen world had to offer. I wasn't going to worry about right or wrong, I was just going to do it all! Consequences wouldn't matter; the experience was what I was going to live for. So I did.

Chapter 10

THE YEARS THE LOCUSTS ATE

I received the title "Life of the Party" in the high school yearbook, and it was my valedictorian moment; I had succeeded in accomplishing what I always wanted to achieve—living each day as a party. I wore that title like a badge of honor because I was always looking for a way to justify my unacceptable behavior. "Well, I'm the 'life of the party,' so therefore..."

I graduated from high school truly by the skin of my teeth. There were parties all summer long celebrating the graduates and going away parties for those heading off to college. I was proud of the fact that I was going to college, and I planned toward it as a foundation for building my new and exciting life. I was accepted into the hotel management program at SUNY Cobleskill Ag and Tech, and I was so excited to begin. It seemed perfectly in line with all of my other friends; I would go to school and learn how to have a career in a field I felt I was designed for. However, even with the most committed of intentions to do the right thing, I lacked the willingness to do my homework or study as much as I could so that I could step into a field and excel. Even though it seemed like the correct "next step" from high school, and I knew college was where I would learn how to succeed in the business, I still lacked a moral compass. The freedom to do whatever I wanted, whenever I wanted to—it was too much of a temptation. I was up against a tidal wave called alcoholism that dictated my reasoning, and although I know that God knitted a heart of hospitality in me, I never invited God into the steps of my journey so He could help me achieve HIS goals for my life. The pull to drink was too much of a riptide, and there was no way to stop the wave from pulling me under. It would be ten years before I escaped the current and crashed on the shore.

As I was finishing my first semester, I realized my grades were suffering. I was put on academic review. My school had a work study program that I was able to take advantage of. I chose the hotel business and was granted a work study opportunity in Houston, Texas, where my brother Ned lived. He was one of my greatest fans. He always spoke of the "possibilities in life," and encouraged me to dream and materialize anything my heart could imagine. He always treated me as an adult.

When I was thirteen, Ned sent me a letter that laid out what it was like living in our family before I was born. No one had ever spoken to me like I was mature enough to receive this hope and encouragement. To be able to begin my adult life with my brother was the perfect launch. I felt that Houston was the perfect place for me, a place where dreams were made, and my brother would be there to help support them along the way. I procured a position at the Dunfey Hotel. It's funny the things you take as a "sign from God." The Dunfey Hotel had its corporate offices in Hyannis, Massachusetts, and since I loved Massachusetts, and my cousin summered on Cape Cod when her family wasn't at the lake house in August, I knew it must be what God's plan was for me.

Once I was accepted into the work study program, and I had all the facts together, I asked my brother in Houston if I could live with him, and he said yes. I failed to mention to anyone that I knew I was failing out of college and wouldn't be back for the third semester. I struggled with this truth because if I told my parents, they wouldn't let me go to Houston, and if I told Ned, he might not let me come. I just moved forward, determined to deal with the consequences when they came. That's a perfect example of how I navigated adult life.

Although I was beyond excited to leave my mistakes and boring life behind, I was still so afraid to leave the security of my mother, who was one of my biggest fans. I did not want to lie to her, but I was too afraid to tell the truth. College was my first break from home, but moving to Houston was a huge step into adulthood. I was afraid and yet also so excited! The tears flowed as I said goodbye at the airport. I was so young and making my way in the world, and I didn't always realize what a best friend my mom really was. She loved me so unconditionally, and she would encourage me to be the best version of myself, even though I always thought I knew better. She was generous, would try to be fun, and would show me the possibilities of everything. She taught by example with a level of grace, sophistication, generosity, kindness, and selfless acts of love through her time and sacrifice. She was "classic!" I wish I could tell my younger self to cherish the time with her.

Chapter 11

THE PATH OF DESTRUCTION

YeeeHaww! I was finally getting out of Upstate New York and moving on to my new "BIG HUGE LIFE" in Houston, Texas. It was a WILD RIDE! The Incomprehensible Demoralization was the theme of this decade.

I landed in Houston at nineteen and loved, loved, loved my job as a hotel clerk at the front desk of the Dunfey Hotel. My brother Ned was incredibly gracious. He would drive me to the hotel by 6:45 AM every day. He had a plumbing business, and Houston was booming! I felt like I was a real grown-up. It was a wonderful time to be a new resident in Houston as it was a melting pot due to the boom. People were moving there from all over the country. The city felt new and shiny. I went drinking with people after work, I lived in an apartment with my brother, I went out to dinner or "lunched." I had ARRIVED!

As I settled into life in Houston, the city swept me up into a tornado that I couldn't seem to control. It was one bad decision after another. I drank in bars all the time, leaving with people I didn't know. I entered into an affair with a married man who became my boss. I was arrested for a DWI as I passed out at the wheel of my car. My behavior became unrecognizable. Who had I become? " Selfishness and self-centeredness—that, we think, is the root of our troubles. Driven by 100 forms of fear, self-delusion, self-seeking, and self-pity, we step on the toes of our fellows, and they retaliate" (*Alcoholics Anonymous,* pg. 62). Boy, no truer words were a better description of my behavior during these years.

As I got lonely and felt lost, I took a hostage: my sweet Bob from high school. I presented promises of this beautiful life together. I knew he was not happy in his life in New York, so I dishonestly manipulated him to make a huge life change into my world, which was an unstable existence I needed saving from. Once again, I wasn't concerned about the other person and their needs. It was ALWAYS about looking for a savior for me!

Bob took all his savings and moved to Houston. It was a party for quite awhile. I was working, he found work, and we tried to act like two mature adults, but alcohol and pot were constant companions, and I wasn't able to see the blessing I had in this lovely man. I was literally drunk or high when I wasn't working, and I started to interpret his fear of the crazy life we were living as being needy and weak. When he couldn't provide me with the comfort and support I selfishly needed, I discarded him, leaving him in Houston with no friends or support other than the people he worked with. I can still recall the sadness and disbelief when he said, "Kathy, don't do this," but I was too self-absorbed and shut down to any moral compass to think of anyone other than myself. I walked out the door with a pit in my stomach, knowing that my behavior was cruel and that I was leaving him to fend for himself. I would rationalize my behavior with the help of drugs and alcohol. I played with the lives of people to suit my needs, and if they didn't meet my expectations, I discarded them. I literally broke every commandment there was. Where was the little girl who never wanted to break a commandment?

Just when it seemed like I couldn't get any lower, I left a bar one night and pulled up to a stop light. It was late and I was drunk. I passed out at the wheel, and a kind soul came up to the window and knocked. I came to, looked at the person knocking on the window and bolted through the red light. At that same time, a police officer came upon the scene and pulled me over. He gave me the sobriety test, which I failed miserably, and he took me in to the station. They booked me into the Harris County Jail. They put me in a holding tank, and it was rough. There were prostitutes (they actually took care of me), other drunk drivers, and a woman who was in for assault (she didn't like any of us and basically terrorized us all). There I was in my little pink shirt and jean skirt, not looking like I belonged (or at least that's what I thought). I kept trying to get a phone call, but there were others before me. I prayed, of course, that this was just a dream. It wasn't.

I didn't get to make my call until the wee hours of the morning. I called my brother Ned, and of course he came to pick me up. I think one of the most disturbing elements to this story is what followed. I convinced myself that this was a rite of passage. I didn't have any remorse; I just chalked it up to an experience everyone should go through and picked up a drink that afternoon. My drinking had gotten way out of control. I needed help, but I had no idea I did. At that point I was no longer at the hotel. I was working at Ramset Power Actuated Tools, and the company vehicle they gave me was impounded. Again my brother came to my rescue and helped me get it out of the facility. His generosity and kindness was all I could have ever hoped for, but I knew I was taking advantage of his kindness. As usual, I was desperate, so I pushed aside any sense of pride or personal code of dignity. I asked without acknowledging the reality that he did not need to be my financial escape. If I hadn't gotten help from him, I would have gone to jail, which is where I should have gone, but God's mercy blessed me yet again. I did not think I could sink any lower than I was, but the depth of my selfishness and ability to lie to my loved ones had reached an all-time low.

Houston, Texas; Cape Cod, Massachusetts; back to Utica, New York; Acton, Woburn, Medfield, Massachusetts; Queechee, Vermont; Charlestown Massachusetts . . . . The following years stripped me of any moral fiber I might have had left. The enemy knows how to do this masterfully—a steady drip of shame, embarrassment, and incomprehensible demoralization. As my alcoholism progressed, the experiences became like a revolving door of unconscious decisions, coming to, and turning the whole demoralizing experience into a joke. I constantly spoke degradingly about myself, with humor of course. My drunken indulgence left me feeling remorseful: how could I have (fill in the blank)? I learned to act as if I had it all together when I really hated myself for my unacceptable behavior, actions that I would never let a friend experience. The inability to ask for what I wanted, like protection in sexual acts (What if he won't like that? What if he doesn't like me after that?), was like a gag on my mouth, although it was a gag I put there. I was vulnerable because I put myself in vulnerable positions. I was not "taken advantage of" because I was the one who had an agenda. I wanted to find the partner who would "take care of me." I was wanting a fairytale experience. Meeting the partner who is designed for me usually doesn't happen at midnight when I am incapable of making clear decisions, when I'm not coherent enough to qualify the character of the man in a drunken state. Instead, I freely gave my God-given gift of sex to a stranger, all because I was desperate to be found, seen, accepted, and wanted. It's funny how you think, "This will be a new beginning, a new adventure that will turn my life around," but nothing changes. And if nothing changes, you're left with the same behavior and problems, just in a different surrounding.

Chapter 12

EXIT STRATEGY

I had to go to court for the DWI. The judge was merciful and gave me probation and a fine. Again, my brother helped me with my circumstances. I was working, so I could pay him back, but I wasn't taking responsibility for my actions or my financial irresponsibility.

One of the conditions of probation was that I couldn't leave the state of Texas without a job in another state. I knew it was time for me to leave Texas and try to get a grip on life, so I talked with my cousin Grace and explained my circumstances. She always saw the good in me and had a protective spirit about my indiscretions. She offered to get me a job as a waitress for the restaurant company she worked for on Cape Cod, and I could live with her and her friends. I left Texas, miraculously ALIVE.

It told myself that this time it was going to be different!

I moved to Cape Cod. My cousin and I would be moving into the new house with her friends at the end of the month. In the meantime, my aunt and uncle, whom I adored, graciously offered for me to stay at their beautiful summer cottage on Cape Cod, with one request—not to touch the boat and not to have anyone at the cottage. Of course I wouldn't touch the boat, and I didn't know anyone, so guests wouldn't be a problem. Unfortunately, at this point in my life, I was incapable of being trusted with anything, and my word was just words for me to get what I needed. I never had malicious intent to break my promise or cause trust to be broken or to harm the people I loved and cherished, but as an alcoholic, I had no control over what I was doing. The conflict of who I was and who I actually wanted to be was a battle going on inside me that I couldn't break, and I didn't want to. When I wasn't inebriated or high on drugs, my alcoholic behavior taunted my coherent young life. I learned much later that an alcoholic has an obsession of the mind.

I moved my things into the cottage and started working. I got to meet the crew that Grace had been working with for the past two summers, and I drank every night. As I did, I found my people—my co-workers partied like I did. These were the people who lived on the cape year-round; the summer staff did not arrive until Memorial Day weekend. Just before Memorial Day, a couple of the guys I worked with came over to the cottage (broken promise number one), and as we got drunker, the suggestion came up to take the boat out and just "pop over" to one of the guys' house. I told them I didn't think it was a very good idea, but the guys assured me they had done this with my cousin Grace. Eventually, I agreed, and off we went. They seemed like they knew what they were doing, but I had no experience. I knew nothing about navigation, tides, or mooring a boat. We took the boat into shallow water and got out to go to our friend's cottage where he had more pot. We stayed there longer than we anticipated, continuing our drunken spree. When we went back to the boat to head back to my aunt and uncle's, we discovered that there's this thing called tides, and if you don't know how to handle the times, then you can run a boat aground!!!

Oh, the sick feeling I had was almost too much for me to bear. How could this happen? NO, NO, NO . . . that familiar cry to God. I had the feeling in my stomach of impending doom; it was like a nightmare that I couldn't wake up from. Please, oh please, make this a dream. What will I do? We had to call the Coast Guard, and that experience in itself was too much. We had to lie about whether we were drinking or not, there was confusion about the license and registration and what address they were towing us to and who was responsible (the boys actually handled that part, which was very helpful). The Coast Guard pulled the boat up to the dock. I knew that I had just made an irreparable mistake of enormous proportion. I was afraid I had ruined a divinely orchestrated relationship with my precious Uncle, who always encouraged me. He would say things that told me he saw the possibility of me being the woman I had hoped to be, even when I didn't bear any resemblance to her.

I lied to my cousin and avoided my aunt and uncle when they arrived at their house. The house was clean and the boat in place. I was so consumed with how I could cover it up by cleaning the boat and trying to do things that would "cover my tracks" that I never thought about the neighbors who saw the boat being towed by the Coast Guard. When I went to see my uncle after they arrived for the summer, he was furious, and rightfully so. My cousin was bewildered. She always saw the best in me but didn't see this coming. Lying to her and to her parents was one of the cardinal rules you didn't break. The embarrassment and shame I felt was palpable. Aunt Ann had come to visit me at the new house when they first arrived, and I said nothing about the boat incident, although she already knew from the neighbors. I'm sure that broke her heart as she probably came to bless me with the opportunity to tell my truth. Lies of omission are just as harmful as bold-faced lies.

When Grace told me they knew about the incident, I asked if I could come over to talk with them. My uncle explained how disappointed he was and that when they came down, the first thing his neighbor asked was, "How's the boat?" He spoke sternly, but he didn't say he was done with me. I was grateful for that. I apologized to my aunt as well and told her I hoped she could forgive me. She said it would take some time. Eventually, my uncle did forgive me, and we had a special bond. I never did ask him why he did; all I know is I'm eternally grateful that somehow he did. My life would truly not be the same without his encouragement and belief that I could "do better." I have no idea where my life would have ended up without my uncle and my cousin Grace's unconditional love.

Despite the boat incident, the summer was a continual party, with one blackout after another. I worked and drank. I was never alone, but the difference was the others stopped, and I didn't. I spent rent money on drinking and drugs over and over again, and my gracious cousin would help me out. By Labor Day, the party, as they say, was over. I went back to Utica, New York, to my parents' house and got a job at the Sheraton Utica as a cocktail waitress. It couldn't get any better for me. Cocktails, drugs, music—it was all there, an alcoholic's dream. I did not want to be back home. The only thing that made it bearable was the drinking and smoking pot Every day, all day. I felt like I had gone to hell. After two years of living in an alcoholic fog in my hometown, I had to get out and get a life that was going somewhere. I had no interest in settling in Utica, so it was time for me to move on. I needed a change! Then one day I was talking with Grace, and again my angel in cousin-form said, "Why don't you come here? I'm sure my parents would love for you to come and live here until we can find a place of our own!" This was my ticket out . . . a new start!

When I got to Massachusetts, I couldn't believe it. I had a real new beginning. I was with my favorite people and the one person I wanted to be "just like." I was going to be able to live with her, and we'd build our careers and lives together. It was a dream come true!

In my mind, everything was possible. They lived in Acton, Massachusetts, right next door to Concord. It was so beautiful. The stone walls, rolling hills, horse farms, gourmet farm stands. This time it was going to be different. This time, I was going to get my life together. It was a new beginning. Could it be possible? I was going to give it my all!

Grace was already working at a hotel bar that served food. They were looking for help, so I was instantly employed. Of course, I loved the bar environment. I automatically gravitated to my people who drank like I did and drugged like I did. I would do lines of cocaine in the bathroom every shift. I knew it was a problem and that I was spending too much money on it, especially since I needed money for a deposit for the apartment with Grace. I loved the bar and the people, but I knew I was destined for more.

In June, 1986, basketball star Len Bias died from heart complications due to the use of cocaine, only two days after being drafted by the beloved Boston Celtics. That caught my attention! Here was a guy who had done everything to achieve the dream of a lifetime, and it ended because of drugs. I was on that same trajectory to death if I didn't do something about it. That was it; no more cocaine. Of course I still drank and smoked pot because, well, they weren't as harmful! The insanity of my addiction was real! How I felt like I was actually taking the high road is such a joke. But God is gracious.

I loved the hotel business. Grace thought I would be great in sales. I felt like my life since high school had been a blur—and it was—but she helped me take the pieces of the broken road and come up with a pretty solid resumé. As I put down my experience, I saw I actually had a good amount of it, but my disease didn't want me to feel that way. The hotel was looking for an outside Corporate Sales Manager who could develop relationships with the local companies and provide the Corporate Assistant with a point program that rewarded the company with complimentary guest rooms, dining vouchers, and accommodations at one of our other properties on Cape Cod or Martha's Vineyard. I would be the liaison between the hotel and the Corporate Assistant. Oh, it was such a perfect opportunity! Please, God, I just need a break. I'll do better, I promise!

I GOT THE JOB! Wow! I couldn't believe it. I got paid thirteen thousand dollars a year, which was what my mother made working in the Physical Education field her whole career. I just couldn't believe it! I had finally done it . . . I got my life together! My parents were so proud and I'm sure a little relieved. I got busy and designed and implemented the rewards program; it was a great success! So much so that after a year, I had the opportunity to step into another role as Regional Association Manager. The hotel group had grown with the purchase of hotels in Martha's Vineyard, and they built a hotel in Taunton, Massachusetts, refurbished an armory in Portland, Maine, and of course there were the original Hyannis properties and the Westford property. It was a wonderful portfolio to represent! I was so blown away that they would choose me. I was truly honored and excited to feel like I had made the grade. I was growing in my career, and I was traveling as a representative of the hotel chain. However, alcohol was still a constant, and I was progressing further and further down the rabbit hole of insane decisions. My blackouts were continually causing me to cycle the feelings of shame, self-hate, and embarrassment.

My morning routine, wherever I was, was coffee first, care for the hangover, and take a shower because I always felt like I had a film on me—the alcohol wreaking havoc on my nervous system and pores. If anyone commented on my hands shaking, I'd laugh it off and say, "Wayyyy too much coffee." Then my job was to fish for the details of the night before because I usually had no idea what had happened. I made phone calls to my friends I was with or that I would be meeting at work. It was an awful roller coaster of emotions.

Although I had achieved a position of upper management in the career I loved, the feeling of pride wasn't possible because the ugliness of my alcoholic life didn't allow it. Alcoholics are funny individuals. They present with over-inflated egos but low self-esteem! What does that mean? I would walk into a room with such confidence on the outside, while inside my head was screaming, "You are a con. You have no right to be here. You never graduated college. Your outfit is wrong, your hair—oh my gosh, can you do something with it?" Then I would head straight to the bar and take that liquid courage. I would feel the sigh (aahhhhh), the shoulders would drop, and after a sip or two, I would feel like, "You can do this. Let's go." And that was all it took, that one drink, and I was off. Alcohol was in charge, and I prayed I would not black out that night. The irony of this life is I didn't realize it was the alcohol. I was entertaining to be around and was mostly a self-contained mess, until I wasn't!

I took advantage of the company by making long-distance calls. Remember this was the 80s, and we still used landlines. Phone companies billed for our long-distance phone calls, and my company would chalk my charges up to sales calls. The reality was, it was stealing. Then there was the sidebar drinking on the job and using the company credit card. I'd go out for lunch to the Chinese restaurant down the street with my colleagues who drank like me, and we would have a scorpion bowl (straight alcohol) and wouldn't return to work. Or if we did, we would probably reek.

The last straw was the night I went out to an MPI (Meeting Planners International) and met the sales crew at the bar in downtown Boston. I didn't drink at the event because by this time I knew that if I started, I would get sloppy, so I was meeting my friends later. I had two glasses of wine and headed home. The officer that pulled me over said I was going the wrong direction to my home, although I insisted it was the next exit up. I was on 93 South, but my way home was 93 North. My second DUI! Yikes! My cousin came and bailed me out. I wish I could tell you anything about that night, but I have no recollection of the details. I don't recall anything that happened in the jail, nothing. I went to court, and I actually hired a lawyer because I knew with the second DUI I could probably lose my license. The thought of that was too overwhelming! I couldn't imagine that happening, and I was desperate to get someone to help me. Please, God, I know there has been A LOT of pleading for help! How was I going to get to work? I was so ashamed. Another embarrassing mess.

While I was waiting for my court date, I took the train every day to work, but it was not easy. Once I finally accepted commuting, I did enjoy my morning ride. My lawyer was great! He was a big Irishman who understood my situation. A fine Irish lass such as myself would have no problem with having only a couple of glasses of wine. He took that tack and said he thought I had been slipped a mickey. The truth was, I was drunk! But I was desperate, and he asked me to trust him. So I did. He got me off with only the remaining days leading up to six months, and then my license would be reinstated. Sadly, this had NO IMPACT on my drinking whatsoever. My life was just a broken trail of lies, disappointments, selfishness, and self-centeredness.

I felt like I had better get a handle on my drinking, so maybe I needed another job. I loved being able to say I was the Regional Association Sales Manager. It made me feel so important, but a title didn't excuse my irresponsible behavior. It certainly didn't make me feel authentic.

Chapter 13

WRECKAGE

Unfortunately, my behavior followed me from hotel chain to hotel chain. I had made a name for myself as an outside sales rep. I developed great relationships with my clients, and I had a basic instinct for hospitality. I could anticipate the needs of the client who was referring their employees to us as well as meet the needs of the guest that would be staying with us from that referral. I was blessed for most of my career; my executive managers would listen to my suggestions and make the proper accommodations for both. All looked good on the outside, but I continued to drink to inebriation every time I could.

A wonderful job opportunity presented itself as a Director of Sales in White River Junction, Vermont. It was a Holiday Inn that was a part of a small group of hotels in New England. The title of Director of Sales was exactly what I needed for my resumé, and a geographic change was what I needed to escape the reality that I was a mess. A fresh start. Yes, I'll get my life together there. This time it's really going to be different. For a while I was focused on work, setting up the office in a way that would make sense for me. I had a beautiful assistant named Bonnie who loved Jesus, and I am sure her prayers for me are what kept me alive. She would write notes of encouragement, and she would pray for me.

She knew I needed a relationship with Jesus and not just a faith that He existed, although that is enough sometimes for the most profound changes. She would leave notes of scripture, and she blessed me with a Christian daily devotional book by Oswald Chambers which showed me life in Jesus in such a deeper way. Sadly, I still drank every night, then showed up to work shaking and with bloodshot eyes, all the while trying to present as though I was "just fine." I am sure I did not make her life easy.

The hotel hired my friend Shuby to be the front desk manager. She was a gift of companionship, and we always had so much fun together. Now that I had my friend, we were off and running. I finally had a drinking buddy that would make it fun to explore the local watering holes. She was amazing at her job, confident, clear-headed in an emergency, and she knew the front desk inside and out; you wanted her on your team . . . always! We loved our boss; he was a kind, witty, fair, and smart General Manager, and his wife and family were just as lovely. I'm sure they were horrified with my escapades. I justified my inexcusable behavior and drunken escapades with, "There truly wasn't anything else to do BUT to drink."

Again, God's grace placed me in safe environments so I could be protected. From whom, you ask? From myself!

The pattern of my life was that I would reach a place where I had exhausted all my relationships. I would get to the point where my alcoholism was showing. I became a master of disguise, and when I thought others were seeing the truth about my drinking, I felt I had to leave. I reached that point in Vermont; after a year and a half, I knew it was time to go. The wear and tear of my drunken behavior was to the point of exhaustion—on everyone—and it was time to leave.

I started looking for a job. I had an interview with a private hotel group in Framingham, Massachusetts. I had a live interview on my way to Newport, Rhode Island, where Grace was working for a hotel that had just opened up. Another fun place to drink. I would visit often. I met with the Director of Sales, and he was wonderful. I felt as though we hit it off and that it went well. Well, we would see, but in the meantime, it was time to drink!

I was heading to Grace's apartment in Newport. As always, we stepped into a zone of comfort that is very difficult to describe. We always picked up as if we left each other the day before. Ease and comfort is always what Grace brought to me. I always felt better and hopeful when I was spending time with her. I told her about my interview, and she had news of her own. She was getting a job with Dun and Bradstreet and was also going to move back to Boston! WooHoo! Roommates again. There was no one else in the world that I would rather be living with than my cousin! Cheers to new adventures!

The Castle in Framingham hired me as the Corporate Sales Manager. It was a wonderful opportunity and another geographic change, but I couldn't outrun my alcoholism. I still brought it with me. I would love to say that things were different on this part of my path of incomprehensible demoralization, but that wouldn't be the truth.

I was excited to "start anew." Back in Boston, Grace and I found a place in Charlestown! Oh, how I loved living in the city. Everything is walkable or reached by public transportation. Charlestown's population was primarily made up of the Irish, so I felt as though I fit in perfectly. There was a bar or a church on every corner! Running was great because you were either at the Charles River or Boston Harbor. It was beautiful, fun, and I was with my favorite person! Just being with her made me want to be better. This time, it was going to be different!

The sales office was big, and I genuinely loved my colleagues. We would go out socially and have a grand time. My boss was the greatest guy, and we all had the sense of family.

After work we would go to The Ground Round, a chain of restaurants that served moderately priced food and drink. It was also convenient. Many a night I drove home in a blackout and "came to" just as I was going to hit a car head-on or the guardrail.

God's angels that He sent over me had their work cut out for them. It seemed like my alcoholism was getting worse, that I couldn't get a grasp on the little details of life. I quit drinking in December of 1989 and thought that would make a difference. I had nothing other than my determination "not to drink," and I supported that decision with pot. Otherwise known as the "marijuana maintenance program." This was NOT sobriety, but I felt like I was achieving something. When everyone else went to the pubs, I sat home and got stoned! I wasn't praying to God for direction for my life. I felt that if I could stop drinking until St. Patrick's Day, I would prove that I didn't have a drinking problem. I had plans to go to Utica and spend St. Patrick's night with friends from high school and stay with my brother Bob.

I felt this was such a "big deal" while I was on this sojourn of not drinking. I would prattle on about my life without alcohol to Shannon, the Catering Director at the hotel. Her husband was an alcoholic, and she was in Al-Anon. I think I told her I was getting high, but I thought that was better than drinking. It seemed like she really understood me, and the more we shared, the more I would open up to her, revealing little bits of the problems behind the scenes that I wouldn't share with anyone. Shannon was a true friend.

I made it to St. Patrick's Day, three whole months without alcohol. Oh, how I love St. Patrick's Day! It brings me such joy! That year (1990), I went to my old friends Paula and Tim's farm in the morning, and we all got ready to head to the parade in downtown Utica. Part of getting ready was shots of Jameson Irish Whiskey and smoking pot as a chaser . . . along with coffee, of course! Off to the parade we went, donned in our Irish green outfits and paraphernalia. We made it downtown and parked around the Spilkas Bar. We loved Spilkas because they had the best cherry stone steamed clams and $.25 beers. As I was ordering a couple of glasses of beer, I heard, "Big R!" It was short for Big Red, and only my brother Peter called me that. We embraced, and I was so happy we got together before we kicked in to St. Patty's Day shenanigans! Of course, I bought him a beer, and we put our plan in place for the end of the night. I was meeting up with my friends from high school in New Hartford, and he was meeting friends and hanging downtown. Peter knew all my friends, so we all went out together. I was really excited to be staying at Peter's later as it would give us a good amount of time to catch up.

Off we went, and I had a blast catching up with old friends from school. Before I knew it, I had to head back to Spilkas. I walked in and heard "Big R!" We played a few rounds of pool and had a few beers, then we headed to his place. It was one of those special nights. We just talked and talked, laughed, and listened to our favorite music together. I didn't want the night to end. Peter was loyal; he had a heart for the underdog, he would help anyone, and he was a great listener with a great sense of humor. I had the privilege of being his big sister, although I was so self-centered, the conversations usually revolved around me.

This night was special. It would be one of the sweetest gifts to carry me through the hard times to come. We got up the next day, and he went to our parents' for dinner while I headed back to Boston.

"Love you, Big R!"

It just rang in my heart. I love you too, Peter.

Chapter 14

LOSS OF A LIFETIME

I love pomp and circumstance! I was excited to receive an invitation to a special event:

Tom Flately

requests the honor of your presence to

an appreciation dinner

and reveal of the newly renovated

Framingham Sheraton Tara Hotel

May 3, 1990

Tom Flately was the owner of the line of hotels I worked for. The VIP guest list included Boston event planners, travel agents, concierges, the executive teams of our sister properties, and the corporate headquarters team that managed the hotel division of the Tom Flately empire. Not a detail was missed. It was an elegant affair with beautiful linens, centerpieces, place cards, and passed hors d'oeuvres. The napkins were fanned on the charger plate, there were glasses of water with lemon at each place setting accompanied with the four different wine glasses to pair with each entree. It was the kind of setting that I imagined I was made for.

As I stood there admiring the beauty of the room, the table drew me in with a sense of belonging; the forks lined up to the left and the knives lined up on the right, along with spoons and appetizer fork, with the dessert fork and spoon for coffee above the plate. The floral centerpieces, the place card with name, the bread and butter knife to the left—perfection. My mother was raised with pomp and circumstance, therefore she taught us the importance of table etiquette and how to carry ourselves in such a setting. Growing up, we would never put our elbows on the table, never speak with our mouth full, and always chew with our mouths closed. There would be consequences if any of those simple rules were broken. Proper dinner conversation was never boisterous; it was educated, but we were told to stay away from politics and religion. We always placed our napkin in our lap and set the table with the salad fork first, knife blade facing the plate. I thought how proud my mother would be if she could see me tonight.

I was raised to "act like a lady," however, my mother's foreboding words, "Why can't you just act like a lady?" rang true that evening. The night exuded a sense of royalty. My mother taught me that you are to mingle not only with those who are your superiors but also those who are colleagues, and be gracious to those who are serving you. She taught me to have a graceful demeanor and never be loud and suggestive. My behavior that night, unfortunately, did not reflect how I was raised. I decided to start with Vodka Martinis, which were really straight vodka with lemon, which ended that illusion of ladylike behavior as they went down, one after the other.

There was another party going on in one of the suites upstairs, and I was going from the ballroom to the suite. In the suite, I was doing lines of cocaine and drinking champagne. As the night progressed, instead of impressing Mr. Flately, I was sinking into the drunk that no one wants to be around because they are messy. My delusional self felt the added drugs would keep me alert, engaging, witty, and fun throughout the evening. Instead, I was an embarrassment to my Director of Sales, my Sales Department, my Executive Team, as well as myself. I showed no respect for the honor of being invited by the owner of the company. I only looked at it as another opportunity to allow me the right to drink and drug the way I wanted to. It was a distortion of reality that I resided in for sixteen years after I picked up my first drink. I didn't have a say in the matter; the alcohol was in charge!

In my drunken state, I was not the young lady my mother would have been proud of. The reality didn't match up to my dream of my place in this event. Instead, as the alcohol rose to my head, my composure left my consciousness. Instead of gracious conversation, I was loud, using my sarcasm as a weapon with my colleagues. I was making inappropriate jokes that, well, a lady would not be making. With the owner of the company nearby, I thought I was charming and witty, but instead I was loud and inappropriately sharing stories laced with foul language to accent my points. I was the guest at an event that was supposed to be representing the best of this man's company, and instead I acted like I was in an Irish pub.

My father always said if you're using foul language, it's a sign of ignorance. Couple that with slurring my speech and acting tipsy, and you can imagine how this man must have felt witnessing my drunken behavior. I wanted to be acknowledged by Mr. Flately for being an outstanding Sales Manager who worked hard to get to the Corporate Sales Manager position of his prominent hotel chain, but instead, I was acknowledged for my drunken behavior. The young woman who wanted to be seen as a lady with business potential who, through hard work, a pleasing personality, and common sense, was at the launching stages of her career was identified— in this moment and many others to follow—by a disease she didn't know she had. My inability to control my drinking and drugging controlled how I was perceived.

Mr. Flately graciously asked the bartender to stop serving me. I was still allowed to stay for the dinner, just not to be served alcohol. Instead of taking the cue to stop altogether and humbly apologize, I continued to drink on the "QT" in the suite upstairs.

The difference between a "normal" drinker and a "real alcoholic" is that embarrassment would be enough for a normal drinker to stop and evaluate their drinking behavior. A real alcoholic takes the incomprehensible demoralizing situation and makes it about the other person. They never look at the behavior they are displaying. When the dinner was over, I continued partying in the suite throughout the night. As 5:00 AM rolled around, I did my last line. I had to go home to get ready for work as the dawn was breaking.

The first message on my answering machine at home was, "Kathleen, please call. Something terrible has happened!" There were ten more messages just like that. I called my parents' house.

"What happened? What's wrong?"

"Peter was killed in a hit and run accident."

WHAT? NO, NO, NO. It just couldn't be. I had just talked with him over the weekend. He was all excited about his trip to Yankee Stadium with work colleagues on Friday. I couldn't breathe, I couldn't believe what I was hearing. HOW? I couldn't comprehend anything. Reality was altered. Life as I had always known it had changed forever.

My parents said something about him leaving the bar, it was raining, an SUV drove over him and dragged him. I was on the floor, trying to breathe and praying this was just a dream. They asked me if I was sure I could drive. My head was snapping into action mode. I needed to go. Out the picture window of my apartment, I saw my cousin drive in. I ran out of the apartment into the street, flailing like a crazy woman. I told her about Peter, and she pleaded with me not to go to New York in that state, but there was no stopping me. When I am in that place of shock, my only instinct is "to do." I needed to get in my car, turn on the music we listened to, and drive!

I left a message for my boss that my brother had been killed and I didn't know when I would be back. I would need help at Peter's apartment, so I called our friends Terry and Paula and asked them to get some of the guys together. We had to get into my brother's apartment before anyone else because he had pot and paraphernalia that I didn't want my parents to see. They said they would "get the crew," and off I went—no clothes packed—reeling from the news, still physically running on drugs and adrenaline! The angels must have been in abundance.

In every card my brother Peter sent me, he always said "Wish You Were Here," a song by Pink Floyd. Over and over again I listened to Pink Floyd. I just couldn't believe what had happened! There were so many questions: Is he ok, ohhh Jesus, is he ok? Jesus, please show me signs that he is ok! I was in complete and utter shock. I just wanted to make sure the angels had him and he was in the arms of Jesus. We were raised Catholic, and I knew he believed Jesus was the Son of God, but did he have a relationship?

Interesting the thoughts that truly matter when you lose a loved one. None of the outside things mattered: a spat, money owed. You are just flooded with the sweet memories and the comfort of knowing that you will see them one day. I stepped into another realm, time and space were out the window. I was in my own world, and nothing seemed to matter but knowing that my baby brother was safe in the arms of Jesus.

At Peter's apartment, we checked the place out. I met the landlord. He wasn't too sure I was legitimately Peter's sister. After presenting the proper ID, he opened the door for us, and Terry and my friend Mark stepped in first. As I was getting ready to enter the upstairs apartment, the landlord fell to the ground at the bottom of the stairs. Really? Is this really happening? I ran down the stairs and saw he was unconscious but still breathing. I jumped into action and called 911. The EMT's quickly responded. His daughter came out of the apartment, and we stayed with him until the medics arrived. He presented as having a heart attack, but they would know more once he got to the ER. His daughter went in her own car, and I walked with her, making sure she would be ok to drive. She thanked me, gave me her condolences, and left!

I finally got to my brother's apartment. Mark and Terry were in the process of gathering paraphernalia, plants, anything that seemed questionable. We packed it all in the car. I knew I would be back again for the rest of his things after the funeral (wait, I'm going to be going to a funeral?). As we searched the apartment, I came across a drawer with needles. WHAT was this? What was really going on with Peter? I was so confused. I would have known if he was doing heroin. As I was frantically trying to make sense of it, I saw a prescription for insulin. How did I not know this? Did he tell me and I just forgot? I couldn't process any more information. As I was outside waiting for the guys to put some things in the car, I felt something land on my shoulder. It landed like a pebble, and as I went to touch it, my hand felt wet. Sure enough, a bird pooped on me. I mean, why not, breaking and entering, man down, and bird pooping on my shoulder. Too many coincidences to not feel as though the angels were with me. I looked up at the sky and started laughing. You little rascal, teasing me still. I took it as a message from my brother that he was with me.

There is so much that we don't know about in the spiritual realm, but what my experience showed me was that I was surrounded by angels of comfort and protection as I was consumed by grief.

Our friends came from all over for the wake. It meant so much that they made the time. Everyone was in shock; he was twenty-six years old with his whole life before him. Peter was a very special spirit. He was thoughtful, kind, funny, and was always there for me. I was not the best sister, as I wanted life to revolve around me. I resented him when we were little because I demanded to be the center of attention. After my older brothers left the house, it was just Peter and me with our parents. When it was just the two of us, I could be a sister who was kind and loving, funny and playful. When my spotlight was threatened, I could also be cruel, excluding him or saying mean things. The sad thing about our relationship was that I would abandon Peter for anything that I wanted to do. As I was drinking at such an early age, I obviously was keeping secrets which did not allow me to be available to him throughout our time at the house growing up.

Unfortunately, or fortunately, we bonded over drugs. I found that Peter was getting high, and of course so was I. I would love to say that we grew together over God, church, Jesus, but we did not. We grew together as we became teenagers. Up until that point, it was ok for me to do drugs, but not my baby brother. I was very judgmental about how I thought he should live his life. I didn't like his friends, and I wanted him to act a certain way and would be critical. As our bond grew, we became thick as thieves while we were together in our parents' house. We ended up having some of the same friends, Terry and Paula specifically. They lived on a farm, a beautiful place with lots of parties in an environment that allowed for beautiful walks, swimming in their pond, riding the horses, loud music, bonfires, and lots of laughter. It was a beautiful escape from reality. We liked the same music, and we would sneak away at family gatherings, get high, come back into the fold, and be altered just enough to have a good time with our parents. What would I do without him? I couldn't believe he was gone.

The services were a blur. I was so self-consumed about MY feelings, never considering how my parents or my other brothers felt or what they were going through. It was ALL about me. So many lovely friends showed up. They shared how wonderful Peter was, and talked about his kindness and generosity. Peter was the guy who would help you move, sit with you if you broke up with your girlfriend, listen to your troubles, and offer balanced advice. He would spend his last dime on you and be there for you no matter what time it was. His friends' emotions were so genuine, I could tell they lost a brother as well. My friends were so kind to me. We had all grown up together. They knew I was completely devastated and wanted me to feel their love and support.

I so appreciated their love and care, the memories that were shared, and the grief they exhibited. I appreciated those who said they knew exactly how I felt because I knew they meant well. But those few who had actually walked in my shoes, who had lost a sibling, they were the ones who gave me hope. I never thought I would smile again. I never thought I could think of him without tears. I never thought that the weight of that pain could ever possibly be lifted. The fabric of my existence was altered, and all that I knew life looked and felt like was forever changed. My brother was not going to call me and share his life or make me laugh until my stomach hurt. Who would sit next to me at the holidays and laugh at my jokes, and all of our little inside jokes that we had were over. The people who had lost their sibling showed me they were living their life. They could think of memories and smile and be grateful for them. I hung on their every word of hope.

At the wake, there were so many beautiful stories of an amazing young man who was tenderhearted, thoughtful, and kind. Through these stories, I had a moment of clarity, and I realized I had missed so much. God blessed me with a rude awakening. I truly saw my self-centeredness for a glimmer of a moment. I was self-centered to the extreme; when Peter would tell me a story, I would think about what I was going to say while he (or anyone for that matter) was sharing the details of his life. I would miss the stories of his life because I was obsessed with sharing the details of my life so that he, or anyone, could tell me how wonderful I was. I would get just enough information on the topic to be relevant with my response, but then I would be consumed with my own thoughts of how I could sound better or think about how that reminded me of something about me. I did it with everyone. God used this poignant opportunity to drive home the loss I had in the lives of those I loved. I really didn't know what WAS going on in their lives. I never saw it until I realized what I lost, and the tragedy was that I couldn't get it back. I couldn't "do better." There was no "do over." Peter was dead, and I only had stories of the man I should have known entirely but missed the opportunity to be a strength and support in his life as his older sister.

The bank that he worked for had a special needs employee, and the mother of the young woman came and told me how Peter walked her special needs daughter out from work every day and really looked after her while she was at the bank. My parents truly instilled in all of us a spirit of service; all my brothers are this way. Peter was born with a birth defect that affected his weight. My parents took him to specialists but had no real answer. He was born premature, and his growth was stunted, so his weight was always an issue. Even at twenty-six he had a baby face and was heavy, but always had a smile.

I woke up the day of the funeral hungover and just raw from the disbelief. It is an indescribable feeling of such a blanket of sadness that settles into your soul, a grief for the life that will no longer be a part of yours. It is unimaginable to think of how you will go on in life; it's utter emptiness. My thoughts were with the Lord; in my despairing state, I begged God to please keep him safe, please welcome him into heaven, please show me a sign that he's ok. He was such a sweet, tender spirit; I still believed that God's plans were for good. Romans 8:28 says, "And we know that in all things God works for the good of those who love him, who have been called according to his purpose."

We went to the family service, and while we were there, I realized Peter didn't have his walking stick. He always used a walking stick when we would go on a hike in the Adirondacks. He loved it there. My thinking focused on that thought, and I became crazy with the belief that he had to have it with him for his new adventure. Only thinking of myself and what I felt needed to happen, I created unnecessary drama about it before we got to the funeral parlor. I had my brother Ned take me back to the house so we could get it from the garage, and then met the family at church. My poor parents. They were probably just numb to my drama. The selfish actions that I displayed that day are so incomprehensible to the woman I am today, but back then, all that mattered was that, in my state of grief, I sent Peter off with all he needed.

The service was surreal. I didn't hear a thing: not the sermon, not the people who said things. I was there, but I just kept looking at the casket and the statue of Jesus with the vibrant red heart. Jesus always gave me such comfort. We went to the cemetery where Peter's body would finally rest. I was still pleading with Jesus to show me signs. We had a gathering at a restaurant after, and I just drank, as did everyone else, but it never helped the pain. It was just an altered state of the same grief. The only space I felt any connection with was when I was talking with Jesus. Peter was with him, not here, so I knew I was closer to him when I was talking with the Lord.

I surrounded myself with his friends and music, anything to feel like Pete was close to me. As we were Catholic, I was so worried about whether I would see him again. What I did know was that my little brother was a good soul, and he knew the Lord. I really should have been more worried about my soul than his.

I had to get back to my life; my boss called me, who was a dear friend, and he and the Director of Catering, my dear friend Shannon, came to the funeral. It meant so much to me. I knew it was time to go back to work. I drove back to Boston praying that God would show me a sign. He gave me a rainbow, which translated in my mind to "Somewhere Over the Rainbow." I didn't know at the time that rainbows are the promises of God.

*"I have set my rainbow in the
clouds, and it will be a sign of the
covenant between me and the earth.
Whenever I bring clouds over the
earth and the rainbow appears in
the clouds, I will remember my
covenant between me and you and
all living creatures of every kind.
Never again will the waters become
a flood to destroy all life. Whenever
the rainbow appears in the clouds, I
will see it and remember the
everlasting covenant between God
and all living creatures."*
Genesis 9:13-15

I believe the promise was that He was with me no matter what. I couldn't imagine I was going to ever feel normal again. I just was going through the motions! Grief is like that. It's a vacuum of your emotions. If you do come out behind the veil of sadness, you are in disbelief that the rest of the world is carrying on.

Chapter 15

BACK TO LIFE

I got back to my apartment on the weekend, and I wanted to go to church on Sunday. My cousin and her new boyfriend came with me. We went to St. Francis Cathedral in Charlestown, Massachusetts. It was a huge Catholic cathedral with seating for probably 1000. Once again, I prayed to God that He would show me a sign. The Gospel reading that day was John 14:1-4:

"Let not your hearts be troubled. You believe in God, believe also in me. In my Father's house are many rooms; if it were not so, would I have told you that I go to prepare a place for you? And if I go and prepare a place for you, I will come again and will take you to myself, that where I am you may be. And you know the way to where I am going."

God is ALWAYS faithful! In my drunken haze, the Lord was answering my desperate plea to tell me Peter was ok, but because I was distraught (and inebriated), Jesus knew I needed more. As I put my hands on the pew in front of me to stand up to repeat the Apostles Creed, I looked down, and carved into the pew between my two thumbs was "Peter." It was a miracle; of all the pews, of all the rows, of all the places I could have sat, I was exactly where the Lord wanted in order for Him to bless me with an answered prayer. He orchestrated it like a beautiful gift, and I received it.

Since I was consumed with the circumstances of my brother's death, I travelled back to the Oneida County Sheriff's Department when they released the police report. I found out that Pete lost control of his motorcycle on the curve, then a car came around the corner of the on-ramp and hit him while he was lying on the ground. It was a hit and run, but there was an eyewitness. The accident happened around ten o'clock at night. As it seemed the Sheriff's Department was not putting any effort into trying to solve the case, I decided to hire my own private detective to see if I could track down the driver. The ramp that my brother wiped out on was one that brought you either to 12 North or to a car dealership on the other side. No one had been interviewed at the car dealership, so we started there.

I was spending a lot of time at Terry and Paula's and traveling back and forth to Boston while my cousin was busy with her now fiancé. It was the perfect time to uncover what really happened. After a few dead ends, my investigator found the car that likely killed my brother. It was taken off the road on May 4, 1990. My brother was killed on May 3. It was black, not dark blue like the eyewitness said, and the person who owned it was the security guard at the car dealership. He worked security on the night shift and would start around that time. Oh, and one more thing, he was a Deputy Sheriff for the Oneida County Sheriff's Department.

*"Call to me and I will answer you
and tell you great and unsearchable
things you do not know."*
Jeremiah 33:3

I scheduled an appointment with the District Attorney in Utica, and she was lovely. Basically, she told me the Sheriff's Department would bury any details so deep into the woodwork to protect "their own" and that fighting it would mostly cause my parents to suffer because it wouldn't go anywhere and they would have to relive the tragedy. She asked, "Do you really want to do that to them?" Of course my answer was no. I left that meeting feeling slightly defeated. As to getting justice, I remembered that God will be the final judge, and I took comfort in realizing that driver will have a hard time escaping what he did. He would have to wake up every day living with the fact that he killed someone. As much as I could take consolation in that, I still needed to let him know that I KNEW.

My detective said we could go to his house to "ask some questions," knowing he was going to lie. I didn't care; I wanted him to see my eyes and to put the doubt in him that he got away with it. We went to his house and knocked on the door, asking if we could ask a few questions regarding a hit and run that took place on May 3. He agreed. I asked about his car, although my detective did not find any hair, blood, or bone fragments when he inspected it (he snuck in and looked over the undercarriage). That was not surprising, since with his profession he would have access to having a car cleaned properly. I didn't care anymore about him having justice; I just wanted him to "see my eyes." The pain, the loss, the grief that consumed me. I wanted him to know that Peter's life mattered! I left his porch feeling accomplished. Empty, spent, but successful in what I set out to do. He knew who I was, a grieving family member who suspected him. I wanted him to feel uncomfortable, and I felt like I achieved that. I could now move on.

God provided me a way to have closure without a dramatic, painful experience at the expense of my parents. He takes care of His lost flock and blesses them in ways they may not understand until they look back years later.

"He heals up the broken-hearted and
binds up their wounds."
Psalm 147:3

Chapter 16

FINDING PURPOSE

Life as I knew it had been altered! I was trying to function. My cousin, the person I relied on the most, was on an amazingly beautiful journey with her soon-to-be husband. Peter died on May 3, and Grace got engaged on May 31. There were engagement parties and showers happening, and then the wedding on October 27, 1990. I wanted more than anything to be present and happy for my beloved cousin, however, I was sinking further and further into my disease of alcoholism. It was a lonely and scary place, and I felt I couldn't let anyone know how bad I was. I don't even think I knew how bad I was. I had "the reason to drink" and be messy—I lost my brother, don't you know.

Being around new life and possibility was not something that gave me a sense of meaning or worth. I was just bitter. Why God? Why don't I get a Prince Charming? I somehow believed I deserved to have a fairytale story because I had lost my brother. I was losing any sense of reality. I was just existing to drink. Every day there was an opportunity, and none more special than a wedding, especially this beautiful event. It was the epitome of grandeur at the Copley Plaza in the Hancock Suite with 200 guests, the breathtaking bride, and the handsome groom. It was all too much to take in. Alcohol was the only thing keeping me together, which was a total lie I told myself. My best friend/cousin was getting married, and all I could think about was myself, what I didn't have, and what I lost. I was filled with self-pity.

I embarrassed myself at my cousin's wedding. I was the worm in green velvet, which is not a good look, to say the least. It was a beautiful wedding; I only wish I could remember it.

Now that the wedding was over, I needed another distraction. I changed hotels and got a job in the city. I wanted to move out of the suburbs, so I was hired as the Corporate Sales Manager for Holiday Inn Government Center. The hotel was located right next to Massachusetts General Hospital, which provided a natural base of business. Corporate was their weak link as they were in need of renovation and someone who would go out and get the business. The hotel business is a small network when it gets right down to it. Boston and the suburbs has a small group of sales managers that are either networking or competing, depending on the person and the property. I didn't have a lot of competitors as we were low on the scale of amenities, so I had to procure new business with sheer persistence, pricing, and personalized service.

As the holidays came, it was such an emotional time. I was home in Amsterdam, New York, with my parents. My brother Ned and his son Stuart came home for Christmas, which was a wonderful distraction. I visited Utica and spent a lot of time at Terry and Paula's. I felt Peter's presence there, and everyone still partied like we did in high school. I felt such comfort being around people who knew Peter, and we would all get drunk and stoned, reminiscing and toasting to him. The weight of his loss was felt by all of us. It was a vacuum of grief, yet nothing I did was relieving the pain. I was still filled with my own selfish feelings, and although I tried to bring a lightness to the atmosphere, alcohol was dictating my every interaction.

New Year's came and went. I needed to find purpose. The drinking and drugging were not working, the sadness was like quicksand, and the music I listened to couldn't chase away the shame and regret.

I had a scary thought—I know what I'll do! I will join the Air Force! The Gulf War was going on, and I thought I could be of service. But first I would have to learn how to fly. *Top Gun* was my favorite movie. The idea of taking off and landing on a ship was a fantasy of mine. In my delusional state of mind, this was going to be my answer. I watched the movie the night before, and on my way to work, I decided that joining the Air Force would give me purpose. I believed God was saying I should do it.

I called Grace and my best friend Shuby and told them I was going to enlist.

"WHAT???" was the response. "I must not have heard you," they both said.

I resented that the weren't supportive of my grand decision. I then proceeded to call the Air Force recruiting office. As I was telling them how excited I was to offer my services in exchange for a pilot's license to fly fighter jets, the recruiter on the other end of the phone asked how old I was. I was twenty-eight, and their age limit was twenty-six. The recruiter apologized, but told me he had a recruiting friend in the Navy. I reminded him I wanted to learn how to fly, not steer boats. He told me they have a great aviation program, so I took the referral and made an appointment to come down after work.

I entered the Navy recruiting office dressed in my blue suit and carrying my briefcase (I wanted to be taken seriously). God met me in the office. As I sat at the recruiter's desk, he asked me a few questions and then said to me, "You don't want to join the Navy." He explained that after boot camp, you are required to live in a submerged submarine. It smells, people swear, and its claustrophobic. He told me he was retiring that day and that I was his last appointment. He'd been a recruiter for twenty-five years. "I am not going to sign you up as my last appointment on my last day," he said. "Go home, talk with your family, and if you really want to enlist, here's another recruiter for you to call. He'll take care of you on Monday."

I mean, WHAT are the chances? If that wasn't God sending His protection, then I don't know what is! I never called on Monday, although I will tell you, if I could do my life over again, I would have pursued a career in aviation.

Aimlessly, I drank and drugged. I would entertain clients at the Holiday Inn and get so drunk, the front desk would ask if I was able to drive home, and they were always amazed when I showed up the next day.

It was now March of 1991. I still was traveling up to my parents' and would go up to Terry and Paula's as well. Whenever I was there, my friend Mark O'Sullivan was always there. We always flirted and had a few "encounters," but now he was married. Unhappily, as he would say. I engaged in the flirting and would get so drunk that any sense of morality was thrown out the window. I needed comfort, and if it came from a married man, then I accepted the challenge. I said he could come live with me in Boston. He did, and it was a disaster. Mark was just another drunk like me. Cute as a bug's ear, funny, but a drunk nonetheless.

Chapter 17

I'm Not Letting Go

Mark O'Sullivan was the brother of Tommy O'Sullivan, my first love. Mark always seemed to be around when my life was falling apart. He was there when my house was robbed and helped us get my parents' things back. He was there now: married, supposedly unhappily. I needed consoling, I needed to feel wanted, I needed to feel better—and Mark made me feel that way. I selfishly took advantage of the situation. Alcoholics love what we call "geographic cures." That is the distorted belief that a new environment will change our life, FIX EVERYTHING, take the desperation of our disease and turn it into hope. I was offering Mark and myself a geographic cure by taking him hostage. I offered to have him move to Massachusetts. Yes, that would make everything better! The reality was, I could no more "take care of" or "help" Mark get on his feet than I could myself. Mark and I were getting drunk, going to dive bars, doing drugs, and I believe God was showing me the cold reality of the path I was on. I knew God had a plan for me, although in that state, I really don't know how I could have "known" anything. In the quiet place in my soul, I knew I couldn't go on like this. I was in disbelief that this was the reality of my life. I was frantically trying to justify my new relationship, especially with my cousin, but she wasn't buying it. She could see the slippery slope I was on, if not with my drinking, for sure with him. I was on such a downward spiral. They say it is always darkest before the dawn, and in my case, I honestly believe that to be true.

Mark and I were struggling because neither of us were responsible, and we only lived to get drunk. The problem was we both expected the other person to be better than either one of us were. We were just two drunks. One night, we had his sister in for the weekend. I was working, and Mark and his sister went to the Black Rose, an Irish Pub in Boston. Mark had basically shut himself off from hard liquor because he "got crazy" when he drank it. Well, he ended up doing shots, and it brought on a whole other side of Mark—the Dr. Jekyll, Mr. Hyde. I came to the pub from work, and there is nothing worse than coming into a group when everyone is already three sheets to the wind. When we went back to the house, Mark was belligerent and called his sister a name that should never be used to describe a woman. I found that unacceptable, and we ended up in a drunken fight. His sister left, and the next day I sent Mark back home on a Greyhound bus to his wife. Mercifully, she took him back gladly. I was so grateful for that. There was just one little lingering detail!

It was now September, and I hadn't had my period. It's amazing I even noticed since I was not grounded in reality. I could not even remember if I had a period in August. I was really slipping. I went to get a test, and sure enough, I was pregnant

. . . again. I was further along than the last time, and I had a small window before it was to be a different procedure. I was just a shell of a being at this point. The progression of my drinking was so severe that at night I would put a chair against my door because I worried that someone would come in and kill me. The enemy had me by the throat. As we know, he comes to steal, kill, and destroy. He was trying to kill me, and if not me, he would settle for the beautiful soul God knitted in me. I had no emotions; the only thing I knew was I was a mess. I couldn't take care of myself, so how could I take care of a child?

I scheduled the appointment and just went on with my life from there. I went to visit some friends, and on my way back, I stopped off at church. I always found solace when I could see the crucifix. I pulled off the road and into this church. I must have gotten the direction from my friends. As I got out of the car, I noticed that it was a circular building. There were pews all around the center of the sanctuary and a huge cross hanging from the center. It was a beautiful church. I sat there, desperately praying for something to make me feel . . . anything . . . hope, I guess? The sermon was on abortion; of course, it was. God was definitely trying to reach me. I sobbed in the back of the church, crying out to God in my head, "I have no business being here, but you are ALL I have. I'm not letting you go!" I believe that was my surrender. I was hopeless. Imagine sitting in church, weeping while listening to a sermon on abortion, knowing your appointment for one was that Tuesday. I left that church feeling like I had a sentence to hell.

I still went through with ending my baby's life. I rationalized and justified my decision. The next day, I was flying to Chicago. I started drinking as soon as I got to Logan Airport. I could not drink the pain away. I tried so hard to get to that place where I was checked out, in a drunken oblivion, but I couldn't get there. My colleague and friend Sam always took care of me. Tonight was no different. I don't remember much of that trip. I showed up, hung over and probably stinking of booze, and then we came home in time for Halloween. It was a terrible rainstorm, and I was beside myself because no one came for "Trick or Treat." I was drinking on the couch, watching *Awakenings* with Robin Williams and Dustin Hoffman. I sobbed at the end after he came back to life only to lose it again. It felt like my life, only it had been a very long time since I felt hope for life to turn around.

I went to the bathroom, looked in the mirror, and gave myself a rallying speech: "Come on, Red, you'll quit smoking, start running, go on a diet, and stop drinking." I looked into dead eyes staring back at me and just started sobbing that much harder. The eyes looking back at me were empty; there was no light. I had said that rallying speech for at least ten years, but I never succeeded. How on earth was it going to be any different this time?

A few days later, my best friend Shuby came to visit. Shuby and I have had adventures, and she loves to retell the stories of our escapades. Oh, how we laughed! No one can get me bent over in laughter like my precious friend. Shuby drank with me and was a constant companion, although she usually stopped drinking midway through the night and would switch to Diet Coke. She was always a trooper and would stay until the end. I was happy to see her; she always made me feel like it would be ok!

This night, she came to visit me where I was staying at my friend's house in Sharon, Massachusetts, and we went out for drinks. We went to the 99 Restaurant, which was a great pub-style bar. The tables or the bar always had pub cheese and crackers as well as reasonably priced drinks. As the night unfolded, and I was going over my troubles that "NO ONE" understood, she listened as she always did. Per usual, she stopped drinking at a certain point, and I, of course, continued. When we paid the check and headed home, I was scouring the kitchen for something else to drink. I had a desperation that Shuby hadn't noticed before, even though we had been drinking together for years. It was at that moment that Shuby had an epiphany!

"Oh my goodness, she's an alcoholic!" She didn't state that to me as I don't believe I was ready to hear that from her. She encouraged me to seek counseling. I had tried it when I got back from the funeral for Peter, but they wanted to talk about my drinking—can you imagine that? I left that therapist's office quite indignant, with a promise to never do therapy again. It's a waste of time and money. However, I was so lost that this time I promised my friend I would explore it.

I contacted Human Resources to see what was in my insurance plan, and sure enough, I had therapy included. God has a remarkable way of divinely orchestrating the most extraordinary circumstances. I only had three psychiatrists to choose from. I asked God to please help me choose the right one and, as always, He answered my prayer. I called the first two and left messages, but on my third call to Dr. Pooley, he answered and scheduled me for that week.

Chapter 18

I'M AN ALCOHOLIC

As I sat in Dr. Pooley's office, I thought, "This is a little extreme, don't you think?" On my third visit with Dr. Pooley, there was an evaluation. He gave me a test. A score of nine meant a person had a serious problem with alcohol. I scored a twenty-three! I had promised myself that I was going to be honest, no matter how much I wanted to "bend the truth" to look better or get my way. Dr. Pooley said that I had two options:

1. **Complete Abstinence.** Well, that was impossible as it was Friday, November 16, and I was meeting my cousin and dear friend in Newport, Rhode Island. The car was already packed with wine coolers and beer, all of which was to be consumed on the ride to Newport.

2. **A Social Agreement.** I would only have two drinks, and if I went over, I had to tell Dr. Pooley.

I chose the Social Agreement. He started to explain that I could have two drinks, no more, and if I had more, I would have to tell him. That's when I realized I had no control over alcohol. I thought, "That's a drop of oil in the engine. I might as well not drink at all!" As much as I couldn't imagine not drinking, I said, "I can't do the Social Agreement," to which he responded that he wasn't an alcoholism counselor, but he would have someone call me on Monday.

Before I left the office, the doctor said, "Alcoholism is a disease. It's not anything that you did to get it. It explains why you did what you did, but there is hope in recovery. We will get you there. Talking with the alcohol counselor will help on Monday!"

I got in the car and took a deep breath, then sighed. That sigh was surrender. Ok, so I really am an alcoholic, in the real sense of the word. It's a disease, so you mean it wasn't that there was just a weakness in me that didn't allow me to follow through on the million and one things I knew I should do? As I drove away, I wondered what the alcohol counselor would ask. Would I have to go to a meeting? I actually felt hope in a way I hadn't before. I don't quite understand that, but the knowledge that I had a "disease" meant there must be a solution. As I drank the wine coolers, I knew that "after tonight, I am done!" I had said that many, many times before, but this time, it truly felt different. I thanked God for His mercy. I turned up the music and drove!

Newport, Rhode Island, has a vibe of fun and frivolity. I was ready to close out my drinking with everything I loved to drink. I checked into the hotel and got ready. It was always fun with Grace and our friend Matt. We then proceeded to drink ALL my favorites. I wanted this "buzz" to be one for the books, but I just couldn't achieve the escape

I wanted. I consumed all my favorites: Quervo Gold, Grand Marnier Margarita, Black and Tans, Baileys. You name it, I drank it. Throw a little karaoke in there, and it was a fitting swan song. That night, when Grace and I got back to the hotel room, I told my cousin about my appointment with Dr. Pooley and the reality of my drinking. I shared how I had hope that I could find true happiness if I was to make this change in my life. Grace was my biggest fan. She always saw the best in me, even when there might only be a glimmer. All she ever saw was the good. She did share that she had noticed a change in me, that I was angrier and sometimes would say mean things when I was drinking. I couldn't deny it. I was miserable inside and blamed everyone for having a better life than I had. Her statement was the final straw. I would never want to hurt or be harsh with Grace in any way. She was my greatest life blessing. I knew this had to stop, and God brought me to the people who could help me do that! I wasn't going to drink again.

November 17, 1991, was my first day of sobriety. I drove home wondering what this was going to look like. I prepared for work on Monday, knowing I would receive a call from the alcohol counselor. I figured he or she would recommend going to meetings. I could do that. I can do this! Monday came, and I went to work sober, with no hangover. I actually felt very good. Clear-headed and hopeful! I couldn't remember when I had felt like that.

The phone call finally came in. I had a conversation with him and took another test. Again I recommitted my vow to tell the truth, even if I didn't want to. I answered the questions honestly, and after he evaluated my answers, he said, "My recommendation is INPATIENT."

"WHAT? That's a little extreme don't you think?" I mean, sure I had a day or two to think about this, and I figured a meeting or something like that, once a week, maybe twice, but INPATIENT? This seemed DRASTIC.

My head was running away with everything that was going to be a problem. "How am I going to get out of work? I have a big sales presentation coming up. They need me. My boss will be furious because I am the Corporate Sales Manager and have to present to our new Corporate Team."

"Ok, BREATHE. Take this information one step at a time. I'll talk with my best friend Shuby, and we will figure out a plan. I'll call my insurance first and see what can happen."

God unfolded the miracles over and over and over again. It's hard to believe. I actually remained sober while I tried to find a rehab. It was a struggle, as every facility said I either had to be "physically drinking" or "suicidal." I wasn't either!

When I was drinking and had gotten myself into trouble, or lied, or felt hopeless, I would wish I wouldn't wake up. That was as far as my suicidal thoughts would take me. (I actually didn't even realize that not wanting to wake up was suicidal until I was a couple months sober and someone in AA spoke about it.) The other issue was I did not know the difference between a detox (that was why they were asking me if I was still drinking and saying they could only take me if I was drunk) and a rehab.

I called my friend Shannon because her husband Finley was sober and had a lot of years in AA. I told her of my quest to get sober and that I had a facility that would take me. I was going down the next day. She said she would talk with her husband and would come with me tomorrow. I trusted Shannon; we had history. She came to my brother's funeral, I went to her wedding (and made a scene). She loved me despite my alcoholism. I was going to go down to a place in Norwell, Massachusetts. I thanked God for the opportunity to change the way I had been living. I asked Him to direct the intake and help me to know I was doing the right thing. I was trusting God completely as I was in a whole new world that I had no familiarity with. I was completely blind, and as Shannon drove me, I was quiet and very pensive. What would it be like? What were the other people going to be like? What would they want to know? Would I have to be honest? About everything? It was a pretty drive by the ocean, and I was grateful for the scenery. It gave me a feeling of hope.

When we arrived, I was filled with fear and trepidation. They had me fill out paperwork and wait to speak with someone in intake. As they questioned me as to why I was there, I answered honestly. I was sober, and since I couldn't enter a detox sober, the only other option was to admit I was suicidal. I was not! I felt like they were trying to trick me with their questions. God's blanket of protection was on me. Shannon was talking with Finley, who had lots of experience helping other alcoholics, and he said, "Get her out of there." So we thanked them for their time and left. I plummeted into despair. What was I going to do now? I had exhausted every opportunity afforded me through my insurance, and all were dead ends. That's the beautiful thing about God's hand in my life. He always gives me blessings that far surpass my minuscule scope of what is before me.

I wanted to go back to my house, but Shannon wouldn't let me be alone. I really didn't want to drink, but I wanted to be by myself. She was not going to leave me alone, so she brought me to her home, and when Finley returned from work, we went to an AA meeting. I don't remember anything that was said, but I remember that I knew I was where I was supposed to be. The noise coming from the meeting was filled with much laughter and joy. I hadn't sincerely felt joy in so very long, it gave me hope. The meeting format was a "speaker meeting," where a member would tell their story and then people shared on the topic. I was so tired from the emotions of the day and week. It was all I could do to try to quiet my mind. I was listening, but I couldn't hear a thing over the noise in my head.

At the end of the meeting, they gave out "chips" for certain lengths of sobriety: 30 days, 60 days, 90 days. I couldn't even imagine staying sober that long. Then they said, "And the most important chip of all. The 24-hour chip or the desire to stay sober." Shannon and Finley encouraged me to go get a 24-hour chip, so I did. I said for the first time, "I'm Kathleen, and I am an ALCOHOLIC." Saying that out loud to a group of strangers felt like it was the scariest thing I had ever done, but surprisingly, it felt right. It was all I could say or do. I felt my shoulders drop, and I acknowledged that I had a problem. I finally knew what the problem was, and as strange as that seems, I had hope that I was accepting help for the problem. The flood gates opened, and I just cried and cried. Shannon and Finley lovingly invited me to stay in their home that night, and I slept on the couch.

The next day was a Saturday. Finley handed me a piece of paper with a number on it. He explained that a friend of his gave him the number at the meeting the night before. He told him to have me call the rehab in the morning and see if they could take me. I had nothing else to lose. Why not? I didn't feel very hopeful since it was a Saturday, but I made the call. I was desperate. I assumed I would get an answering machine, but instead I heard, "Brookside Rehabilitation Hospital. How can we help?" God's grace was on the other end of the phone. After explaining my desire to get help but that all the other facilities wanted me to either be drinking or suicidal, the kind nurse said I didn't need to worry about insurance or anything other than getting to the facility, and they would take it from there. As God (Jehovah Sneaky) would orchestrate, they actually didn't have my insurance plan that day, but they were implementing my insurance plan on Monday. How does that happen? Only God! It was all set. Although I was in an altered state from detoxing and exhaustion, there was no possible way I could miss the divinity in what was unfolding. I could feel God's grace in abundance. I felt like I was in a twilight version of my life, not fully knocked out as I had been while drinking and drugging, but witnessing God's loving hand and an overwhelming sense of peace that surpassed all understanding. I knew I was being taken care of and had no idea how it was happening other than by God's grace!

"Under grace in perfect and easy ways,"—that's how I know I'm in God's will, when everything unfolds effortlessly, all the pieces falling into place without chaos or angst.

Shuby took me to the facility. As we approached, I started to panic a little, but I knew Brookside Rehabilitation Hospital in Nashua, New Hampshire, was the best place to start my treatment. At intake, I promised myself to be honest, which as an alcoholic was one of my greatest challenges. You may be asking yourself, "Why is it so hard for an alcoholic to be honest?" Because of all the actions I did when drinking, I lived in so much shame, self-hate and fear of what others thought of me, perceived or real, that I told stories or bent the truth to put myself in the most favorable light. Just for a moment, I would feel relief thinking that I presented a respectable answer to the other person and they wouldn't know the ugly truth about me.

After I filled out the paperwork, they were ready to take me inside. I said goodbye to Shuby and cried a little as I headed back to the next phase of intake. I was already sober, so they didn't have to physically detox me; they gave me a gown, went through my bag, and took anything that was sharp (razor, scissors, nail clippers, etc.). I only stayed one night in the clinical unit. The next day, I met with a counselor. I explained to them that I was going to have to leave early as I had a big presentation the following week. I believed I was so important that nobody could do the presentation except me. As it was a weekend, the counselor told me I could take it up with the weekday staff.

I remember feeling like I could do this on the fast track. I would be so focused on getting well. Just tell me what I need to do, give me the Big Book and tell me what you want me to read. I'll do it!

The days were filled with structure. Morning meditation reading out of the 24-hour a day Hazleton book, then a class about the disease of alcoholism, group counseling, lunch, more group counseling, followed by one-on-one counseling. I found out I was an emotional mess. I released all the feelings I had stuffed all those years, coupled with the unmediated grief of my brother's death. Drinking had been my solution to all the pain. I had never talked with anyone about what was really going on in my thoughts because I didn't want to face them myself. I tried to silence them through drinking and drugging. What I found remarkable was when the other patients were sharing their journey, I could identify with their feelings. Not necessarily the circumstances, but the underlying pain that brought my disease to life. It was mind-blowing. I wasn't alone!

I explained to my counselor that I was there for the week. My counselor told me it was for thirty days. Well, obviously I couldn't do thirty days; I had a big presentation, and I was *sooo* important. The counselor advised me to think of myself as if I was in ICU. If I had a heart attack, I would not be going to work, and "they" would "figure it out." I responded with my battle cry: "BUT you don't understand! How can I tell them the truth when I told such a lie?" Once again, my self-reliance reared up, trying to keep myself looking good and in control of my circumstances.

I had lied to my boss and told her I was going to Houston, Texas, to visit my brother for the Thanksgiving holiday, thinking I could figure out how to stop drinking and stay sober within a week. It was delusional, but it was real in my mind. Mercifully, one week later, the Lord convinced me to stay. I was engulfed in recovery, which meant I had hope. I was able to surrender yet again. With me, surrender happens in stages. I have to find the willingness to go to any lengths, which is usually preceded by enormous amounts of emotional pain. For me, my emotional pain is the noise in my head telling me that I can't do what God is saying for me to do (usually to tell the truth). What will they think when I tell them I lied? What will they think when they hear it is for alcoholism? Will they fire me because I am not putting on the presentation?

God is always there; He sent His angels to keep me safe and brought me to a place to recover, but I had to be willing to let go of my old ways of thinking that I knew what was right for me. I had to learn that I will feel God's peace when I stop fighting for what I selfishly believe is the right thing for me to do. In this case, I had to call my boss and get honest. I had to call the General Manager and tell them both that I lied and was not in Houston but in New Hampshire, in a facility for alcohol rehabilitation. I truly felt like my world was crashing in on me. I was so afraid of what they would think of me. As I look back on it today, I know that they were actually grateful that I was getting help, but at the time, the disease in my mind was thinking I had let them down because I was such an important person in the company. They handled the news with nothing but grace and loving support. As I surrendered to my thirty-day journey, I ACCEPTED God's plan for me and embraced a willingness that allowed me to be open to the process that would work for me. God knew every detail, and He was there throughout ALL of it.

At Brookside, they also had medical help for those going through detox. When a person is physically detoxing, there are so many things that can happen. In my case, my liver enzymes were dangerously high, and it was swollen. I was actually surprised; I was so out of sync with my body that the pain in my lower back was not even a warning that something was wrong. I just kept anesthetizing myself. Fortunately, I was young and could bounce back fairly quickly physically, much faster than I could emotionally. Others came in with the possibility of alcohol seizures from withdrawal, DT's (Delirium Tremens), or hallucinations. All of these needed to be medically treated and monitored. The physical piece of the disease is the easiest to comprehend (I have an allergy to alcohol/drugs. When I ingest any form of it whatsoever, my body demands more). However, the emotional aspects were much more elusive, especially if you were fortunate enough to still miraculously maintain a job, car, or friends and family. It breeds the lie that self-sufficiency is our solution. For this reason, the psychological team for our disease was much broader. A team of counselors, usually recovered alcoholics and/or addicts, were the real foot soldiers. They had lived the hell we were experiencing and were able to give hope of what life could look like on the other side of the gates. I listened very closely to the people who had "gone through it" as they had full, productive, happy lives. They weren't giving me direction from a book they read, but life skills from their actual experience. I hung on their every word. I knew I could also "have a life" if I was willing to take the suggestions they were providing. They were only asking us to do what they had done to begin their new life.

Substance had been dictating my every move, but now I was going to take a different path. The confidence they displayed through sharing their experience, strength, and hope made the possibility of a new life real to me. That is what won me over. I identified with them when they shared their life in the grips of this deadly disease and grabbed onto the hope that if they could have a new life without alcohol or drugs, why couldn't I? If I was willing to identify with their feelings and not compare my circumstances with theirs, I would receive the gift of hope.

They shared how they experienced the twelve steps. The medicine to heal me was the action of doing the twelve steps that are designed to, upon completion, help me experience a Spiritual Awakening. That process is taking my "faith in God" and developing it into a "relationship with God." It speaks about this in the basic text of *Alcoholics Anonymous*, also known as the Big Book. The solution is so masterfully laid out in the first 164 pages that it has not been touched, and prayerfully won't ever be touched, since 1939. The only way we become properly armed with the facts of our condition is by seeing our Powerlessness in Step One and that self-sufficiency was our god. As an alcoholic, I had to understand that God, as I believed, would restore me from the insanity (doing the same thing over and over again) in Step Two.

In the Big Book, there is a chapter called "There is a Solution." It states: "If you are seriously alcoholic as we were, there is no middle-of-the-road solution. We were in a position where life was becoming impossible, and if we had passed into the region from which there is no return through human aid, we had but two alternatives: One was to go on to the bitter end, blotting out the consciousness of our intolerable situation as best we could, and the other, to accept spiritual help. This we did because we honestly wanted to, and were willing to make the effort" (25).

Only an alcoholic ponders this question. "Hmmmmm. Do I go on like this to the 'bitter end,' or accept the gift of God's hand to freedom from addiction?"

This brought me to Step Three. I now had to "Make a Decision" to turn my will and my life over to the care of God. After seeing the truth about my disease over and over and over again, after realizing the insanity of thinking, "This time alcohol or drugs won't take me to the depths of incomprehensible demoralization," I now had to make a decision to turn my life to Christ. That all sounds good on paper, but I felt like I already had a faith in God and that I already was "turning my will and my life over to His care!" The counselors were so good with meeting us where we were. In my case, I was grieving without a substance for the first time since Peter passed. I had only anesthetized the pain of my feelings with drugs and alcohol. Now that I was clean and in a safe environment, the feelings flowed. The other patients were so kind and comforting when I would share my vulnerabilities. They helped me realize where my "faith" came short.

In the rehab, they had us do a version of Step Four to deal with our "Resentments," but the reality of the fourth step is to see how, over and over again, we were paralyzed by fear and that instead of asking God to direct us or give us the strength to do the right thing, we chose "our way."

This is called Self-Reliance or Self-Sufficiency! It ruled my life. Before rehab, I would wake up with the frightening truth about my reality and that "two-in-the-morning" voice that told me I was "not a good person." I would lie in bed, wide awake, trying to keep up with the lies because I couldn't let anyone know what I was really doing. I believed if they knew the truth, they wouldn't like me. In my head, my distorted thinking told me that I was supposed to act a certain way, people were supposed to treat me a certain way, and when the "play in my mind" didn't come off the way I demanded it to turn out, then I felt I was going to lose something I already had or not get what I wanted.

Another fear that ruled me more than I realized was the fear of what other people thought about me. This frequent fear kept me in a state of restlessness, irritability, and discontentment, and the only thing that gave me relief, at least for the moment, was a drink or a drug. I chased the hope that it would give relief because, at the end, the alcohol and drugs weren't working, which then left me hopeless! It was an endless cycle. The purpose of this fourth step was to flesh out all the shame and guilt that I had been carrying around with me. The direction was to write out all the things that made me angry. In addition to the purging of the resentments, I was to write a "goodbye letter" to alcohol, because the reality was I was in a relationship (as twisted as that sounds) with the substances that gave me relief. Instead of seeking relief from God, I sought relief through alcohol and drugs.

After I read the letter to my counselor (my Fifth Step), I couldn't believe the relief I felt when she said that I had done the best I could do navigating a deadly disease of mind and body! WOW . . . that lifted years of shame off of my shoulders.

Then I asked God to remove the defects of character and humbly asked Him to remove my shortcomings (Steps Six and Seven). Then it came time to make an amends. The only ones I could do that with were my brother Peter and my dad. I wrote letters and read them to my counselor. It was incredibly freeing. So many tears, so much shame and guilt, followed by a feeling that I had never felt before—I felt like I was clean.

The counselors suggested that when we left the rehab, we should get a "sponsor" to navigate life "sober." (What is a sponsor? A person who will guide you through the Steps and teach you, through their own experience, strength, and hope, how to live life without the reliance on alcohol, drugs, or any other substance.)

Chapter 19

RE-ENTRY

I was frightened to leave the safety of the rehab. What would my life look like now? What would the employees at work think of me? Would I want to drink when I saw billboards or felt the call of the bars in Boston? I was desperate to keep what I had found and the possibility of a new life. In my discharge meetings, I had wonderful direction. I asked one of my counselors, "Who will I be without a drink or a cigarette?" They replied, "I see before me three women. One is a wild woman who did whatever she wanted at whatever cost. The second one is a scared little girl who didn't know how to speak up for herself, and number three is a wise woman who kept all of them alive." That resonated with me, because I felt like all three of them at various times in the rehab now that the alcohol was gone.

My other counselor told me to go to an AA meeting the day I got out of treatment. He said that I had to put my recovery first, every day. I used to drink every day, so why wouldn't I go to a meeting every day? I was so desperate and filled with fear that I followed the directions to the letter. He reiterated that out of the twelve people who were going through the journey for recovery together, only one or maybe two would get sober and stay sober. I realized that God blessed me with a new beginning and a new way of life. I was going to do everything in my power to be that "one." I knew it would be a battle, but I would fight for my sobriety. I believed it was truly God's plan for me so that I could become a useful member of society.

I was released on a weekend, so I went to meetings all weekend near where I was living. I reconnected with my family on the phone to let them know I was okay and hopeful for my future. I was grateful to have a little time before I went back to work. Monday came, and I arrived at work, the Holiday Inn Boston right next to Mass General. I was so nervous coming back, but everyone greeted me with such kindness and warmth.

I had to meet with the General Manager, Mr. Prazzi, and he couldn't have been kinder. He said it took courage to admit I had a problem and then do something about it. He allowed me as much flexibility as I needed for meetings. My Director of Sales was just as gracious. She said she felt badly that she didn't know I was having such a difficult time, but I explained that we are good at hiding the mess. As time went on, I heard stories from the front desk clerks who were so worried when I would stagger through the lobby and get into my car in the evenings. They would offer to call a cab, but I always declined. Again, I heard story after story of God's grace in my life. Since I was always in a blackout, the fact that I didn't kill anyone or myself is beyond my comprehension.

It was truly a gift to get sober in Boston. The AA was alive, well, and thriving. I found my people! Now that I had the hope of a bright future, I wanted to find meetings that were attended by people I wanted to model my life after. Successful, happy people living full, big, beautiful lives. The meetings I went to were right in Back Bay (the affluent part of the city), and most of them were populated by executives, politicians, and the elite of the city. That didn't mean that there wasn't a cross section of people, but the meetings I frequented were mostly professionals. It's funny, but you would think if you live in a big city, you would be alone, but the members of Alcoholics Anonymous were everywhere. It was such a comfort to run into someone in a coffee shop, the grocery store, or on the street. When I was drinking, my world got very small. I had only a few people I drank with on the regular, and I wasn't meeting or making new friends who would bring out the best in me. I was gravitating to the people who drank like I did and wanted to hide in the dark. My life was hopeless and lonely. God brought me into a new way of living; the life He would have for me, not the life that was relying on God to pinch hit for me when I was in trouble. I began to learn how to rely on my newfound friends.

Because I still had the emotional maturity of a twelve-year-old, I didn't have the understanding of what character traits I would want in selecting a sponsor. My sponsor would be responsible for taking me through the Twelve Steps in a more thorough way than the thirty days of rehab. The process of choosing a sponsor is very humbling; asking for help was a concept that I was raised to believe was a sign of weakness. In reality, it is a step towards humility. There's a big difference between humility and humiliation. In choosing a sponsor, I wanted someone who had the "look"; I wasn't too concerned about what was inside. My first sponsor in AA came into the meeting with a fabulous outfit and a stunning Kate Spade bag. Now that's what I'm talking about! "Dear God, I want to thank you for bringing me a guide who looks fabulous!" Sarah was an executive in Boston and had a very high-positioned job that demanded a lot of her time. When you are twenty-nine with the emotional maturity of a twelve-year-old and "coming to" from a seventeen-year run with alcohol and drugs, God meets you where you are. I didn't know I needed someone with a strong reliance on God, not someone with a beautiful purse.

Because I was desperate, I took every "suggestion" of the program gladly. Suggestions came from people who had walked this road before me and knew the twists and turns. When I asked for help, they would offer suggestions. I didn't have to do what they suggested for me to do, but if I was honest—despite what my ego would tell me to do—I chose to follow the path someone else took that successfully navigated the obstacle. I realized I didn't need to question the reason for the direction, I just had to do it. This willingness took me through the first blush of the steps up to Step Four, but I didn't know what that was going to look like. My sponsor graciously took me through the process up through Step Five. I don't recall making amends.

There are always lessons when you look for them. In my case, mainly in hindsight, my sponsor was exactly who I needed at the time, even if it was the lesson of humbling myself to ask the question, "Will you be my sponsor?" The asking is what was needed to puncture my ego, which was a valuable process. I'll always remember going to her apartment with the papers that held my ugliest character defects. I truly didn't want these memories to see the light of day. I learned you are as "sick as your secrets," and that it was my alcoholism that kept the lies twirling around in my head and kept me preoccupied with trying to figure them out. My mental obsession was from the fear that generated my thoughts, and that led me to a drink.

After I finished Step Four, I went to my sponsor's apartment, a beautiful brownstone on Commonwealth Avenue. It was warm, sophisticated, tastefully appointed, and comfortable. I imagined if I went through the steps, I too would have the material gifts of the program. At the time in my recovery, it was my only benchmark for success. As we settled in for a long chat, I got out my papers, and we said a prayer asking God to be with us as I shared the underbelly of my life. As I read each portion of the ugliness and pain of the decisions I made in my alcoholism, Sarah would ask, "Did you find this behavior objectionable?" The answer was always yes! The next question was, "Do you see how you couldn't have done it any differently in your own power? That this was the best you could do?" Again, the answer was a resounding yes. Then the question, "What would it have looked like if you asked God for help?" That question made me dig deep. I always felt like I knew what the right thing to do was, but I didn't understand why I didn't do it. Romans 7:15-17 says, *"I do not understand what I do. For what I want to do I do not do, but what I hate I do. And if I do what I do not want to do, I agree that the law is good. As it is, it is no longer I myself who do it, but it is sin living in me."* What was it that stopped me from taking the Godly action versus the selfish one? The simple answer was I'm an alcoholic. I had to mature more through the years to get to a deeper understanding.

For this season in my journey, I experienced a feeling of relief, much like a pressure cooker pushing the nozzle to let a little steam out of the pot. It left a space for me to breathe a little easier. I was so grateful to Sarah for her time, love, and patience. I was going to three meetings a day, and I lived in the sweetest little studio apartment in East Boston. It had a big picture window overlooking Boston Harbor. At night, I would see all the planes lining up preparing to land in this beautiful city. The working fireplace allowed me to have a fire that I could enjoy from the comfort of my bed. It was a home that had the accents that made me feel like it was designed for me (wide, pine, hardwood floors, a kitchen with character and beautiful, slate countertops, and in the bathroom—wait for it—a cast iron clawfoot tub). Oh, how this apartment soothed my soul. It was such a beautiful place to stabilize in.

I had so many firsts. I remember being sick one day, and while I was in bed, I had the realization that I could be alone with my thoughts, and I didn't feel hopeless or anxious. I liked the woman I was becoming. I reflected on all the ways God had been taking care of me. My meetings, my new friends, my relationships that were getting restored. God was supplying everything I needed, and as the noise in my head started to quiet, I could hear the whispers of my heart.

I didn't see my sponsor often; she only went to meetings now and again. God knew that I needed help and provided the necessary guides. When I came into AA in Boston, there was a beautiful woman who scooped me up under her wing. Everyone knew her. She treated the newcomers with love, warmth, and acceptance. She connected us all together by meeting us for dinner after the Park Street meeting at the Golden Goose on State Street. We would go to the meeting and then gather to talk about the meeting and what we were going through. Ellie always greeted everyone with cards that had the Step Three and Step Seven prayers on them, or a devotion she would copy and give to a woman who was hurting, with just the right words or reflections for encouragement. She was truly one of God's special angels, on assignment to welcome the lost, broken, and suffering—someone like me.

Ellie was there for me in such a profound way, acting as a sponsor in the true sense of the word. I talked to her about everything, and she directed me on what to do next. When you come into AA, they say, "Let us love you until you can learn to love yourself." It's a journey. Ellie taught me what that looked like. She brought us into the fold, which is what it looked like to be of service. She would sacrifice time on the phone to talk me through whatever my concerns or questions were, and she met me emotionally with the unconditional love, patience, and acceptance that I had imagined Jesus would have.

My choice for a sponsor was based on my material desires for what I thought would bring me happiness. God met me with a woman who would teach me about love, service, and acceptance. That's the beautiful gift of God's grace in my life. He blesses me with the things I don't even know I need.

Life was amazing now. I was filled with hope and possibility. Some people call this the "pink cloud" phase. I didn't think it would ever end. I felt like I had blessings and awareness that would never have happened if not for the grace of God in my life! So after a time in sobriety, I was contacted by the ITT Sheraton Hotel Boston. The General Manager had asked the biggest meeting planner in the city who he thought was one of the best sales people in the city. I was in rehab when the GM was looking to get in touch with me for the Corporate Sales position for the new Executive Conference Center they were building. The meeting planner for Fidelity Financial in Boston had referred me because I was so persistent in getting him to bring his training to the Holiday Inn Downtown Boston while we were renovating. He said that Fidelity would not have even entertained the Holiday Inn if not for my tenacity. God blesses us in ways we could only hope or imagine. All I did was step into His will, and He unfolded the new paths that He chose for me. In my limited thinking, I just wanted to have a "semblance of a life," but He blessed me with a life, and one more abundantly! The job was mine if I wanted it, and of course, I did! I couldn't believe the miracle of how the job came to be. However, I was loaded with self-centered fear, and I didn't have confidence in myself. I felt like a fraud when they said I could succeed. Recognizing that I never finished college, I was always looking for validation for the work I did. I felt like now I was in the big leagues.

As I got stronger in my recovery, I realized I was "awakening." When I first arrived in Alcoholics Anonymous, the noise in my head was so loud, and I just wanted the noise to stop. Little by little my head would quiet down. I would listen at the meeting to the speaker and notice that it was quiet in my head, first for a minute, then three, then five. It took time, but the noise was quieting down. Just like I craved the alcoholic life, I craved this peace that was beyond understanding. One day I was walking back from my meeting to the hotel, and I always walked through the Public Garden. I used to walk through with such an ache when I saw couples holding hands, or stylish executives walking through, wishing I could be them, have what they had. It was painful. Then one day as I was walking through, for the first time I looked around and saw color. I saw the magnificent beauty of the gardens and the vibrancy of the flowers. I was smiling at people, and they were smiling back. I was happy and grateful, grateful to God for giving me another shot at life. Oh, the possibilities. I felt dreams drop into my heart and thought to myself that I could explore those dormant dreams.

I WANT EVERYTHING . . . EVERYTHING! That song spun around in my mind over and over again. It was a song that I fell in love with from the movie *A Star Is Born* with Barbra Streisand and Kris Kristofferson in 1976. That movie took me captive into a realm of romance. I sang the music over and over and over again! As I was walking through the Public Gardens on yet another beautiful spring day, God dropped into my heart the thought—singing! You have always wanted to sing. Why don't you take lessons? What a concept! Could it be real? Could it be a possibility? Anita Baker was a huge artist at the time, so I used to sing in the car by myself at the top of my lungs. God is in the dream-making business: *"I will repay you for the years the locusts have eaten-the great locust and the young locust, the other locusts and locust swarm—my great army that I sent among you"* (Joel 2:25).

I was off to materialize my big dream. If I was going to become a jazz singer, then I better go to the best. As God orchestrates all our details,

Berklee College of Music was just around the corner from where I worked at the Sheraton. So just like that, I decided I would go to the school and see if I could take voice lessons. At my lunch break, I walked in wearing my little blue suit, petrified and excited all at the same time. The huge atrium lobby was abuzz with the sounds of lighthearted college student laughter and chatter, with ethereal music in the background. It was heaven! I went to the Information Desk and whispered, "I'm looking to take voice lessons." The student behind the desk couldn't hear me, so I repeated louder, "How would I go about taking voice lessons?" The student directed me to Dr. Greenspan, the director of voice. My knees went weak and my eyes welled up as I thanked her. Get it together, Kate! Oh, my goodness, this is really happening.

When I got to Dr. Greenspan's office, he was eating lunch.

"My name is Kate Quist (voice shaking), and I always wanted to sing."

The tears started to flow. He was a little taken aback at my emotion. When he found out I wanted private lessons, he sent me next door to Charlie Santos. As I was sitting outside his office, I couldn't stop the tears from falling. I was just in disbelief that I was materializing this dream, and I was thanking God for His grace and mercy for allowing it to happen. I arranged lessons with Charlie Santos and met with him once a week. The song I chose to practice was the Barbra Streisand song from A Star Is Born. I would practice it every chance I could get.

The lyrics were so perfect for the season I was in. Everything was a possibility, and I was filled with excitement for what God had in store for me!

EVERYTHING

I want to learn what life is for
I don't want much, I just want more
Ask what I want and I will sing
I want everything (everything)

I'd cure the cold and the traffic jam
If there were floods, I'd give a dam
I'd never sleep, I'd only sing
Let me do everything (everything)

I'd like to plan a city, play the cello
Play at Monte Carlo, play Othello
Move into the White House, paint it yellow
Speak Portuguese and Dutch
And if it's not too much
I'd like to have the perfect twin
One who'd go out as I came in
I've got to grab the big brass ring
So I'll have everything (everything)

I'm like a child who's set free
At the fun fair
Every ride invites me
And it's unfair
Saying that I only
Get my one share
Doesn't seem just
I could live as I must
If they'd

Give me the time to turn a tide
Give me the truth if once I lied
Give me the man who's gonna bring
More of everything
Then I'll have everything
Everything

Written by Paul H. Williams and Rupert Holmes
Album: A Star is Born/The Way We Were/Funny Girl 3 Pak
Released: 1976

Chapter 20

THE KINGDOM

Boston is known for its hard winters. This was a huge disadvantage for encouraging clients to host conferences in the city. Boston was competing with Florida, Tennessee, California, Atlanta—destinations with a milder climate. New England is known for NorEasters and unpredictable weather. Event planners would think, "Great city, but would I want to have my attendees struggle with the weather?" Boston in the fall, maybe, but it was not a consideration for a winter conference or even early spring. So Boston got serious about tourism and designed the Prudential Center, which encompassed three conference hotels (Sheraton, Marriott, and Westin), enclosing it all in a "bubble." It was specifically designed so conference attendees could walk from the Hynes Convention Center to their hotels and not be affected by the weather. Brilliant!

Since the hotel I worked for, the Sheraton, was one of the properties inside the bubble, our property had much to gain from exposing the concept to event planners worldwide. I was hired to bring in corporate clients to use the new Executive Conference Center. We worked in partnership with the Greater Boston Convention and Visitors Bureau. We wanted to share with our city all the amenities the Prudential bubble had, so we would invite domestic and international event planners to show off the new construction with all the state-of-the-art amenities. We call them FAM trips (short for familiarization). These familiarization trips showcase the city of Boston, our attractions, the various properties, the Convention Center, and the Prudential bubble, which offers the attendees something to do in rain or shine, snow or heat: a climate-controlled environment. One of the groups the Sheraton hosted was from the United Kingdom. The UK planners were accommodated in our newly-renovated guest rooms, and it was a coordinated orchestration of activities to showcase our city and property in its best light. It was so fun to be part of a team to introduce the planners to the best city in the United States, as far as I was concerned!

As the weekend unfolded, I became friends with a lovely couple who were business partners in England. Our connection started at the beginning of the trip. As the guests had arrived the night before, they had been left welcome packets and an agenda for the weekend, with brochures, gifts of local foods, and a *Where Magazine* highlighting the local restaurants and activities.

Many people think that because they speak English in the United Kingdom they would understand everything we say, but there are certain words that absolutely do NOT have the same meaning. I had one of my most embarrassing moments that morning when all the lovely guests from the UK gathered in the lobby to start our tour through the city, beginning with the famous

Boston Duck Tour. I greeted them with warm introductions and a copy of the day's itinerary, and I asked them if they had brought their fanny packs that the GBCVB provided in their welcome package to make travel on and off the various forms of transportation more convenient. They looked rather confused, so I showed them the fanny pack and again asked if everyone had theirs because it would be useful to carry things around their waist. At this point, my future business partner (although I had no idea at the time) pulled me aside and said, "Please stop saying 'fanny pack.'" When I asked why, she informed me that in the UK, "fanny" means "vagina." Oh, my goodness! I was MORTIFIED.

I turned to my blushing group, as red as a beet, and said, "Well, that couldn't be any more awkward! My apologies to you all!" Well, if that wasn't an ice breaker, I don't know what is. Needless to say, we formed a great bond and had a wonderful weekend exploring the sites of Boston.

I developed a special relationship with Karen White and Mark Seveer. Before they left, they asked if I would be willing to come to the UK to explore joining their partnership. They felt I could help them build relationships with the event planners of the UK and would have a direct connection and familiarity with business done in Boston. Wow. I'd never been outside of the United States, so it was so intriguing to me to be invited to (a) join a company and build a business and (b) travel to another country. I had to pause for about a minute. Thirty-two, single, live in another country and learn entrepreneurial skills while traveling the UK and abroad—a resounding YES! How amazing is my God! I was in such a state of disbelief that He would present me with such an adventure. It was an opportunity I could never have orchestrated.

As the time drew closer for me to leave and I had secured my passport and visa, I was truly humbled that this was becoming a reality. I had created such a beautiful network of friends and support in Boston, and I had now been sober two and a half years. God brought amazing angels who lead by example into my life to show me how to become a woman of grace and dignity. They shared at the meeting about my fear of going to the UK where I would have no friends or accountability, and as usual, God showed up. My little angel Ellie asked her friend to keep an eye on me and meet me at a meeting. I was not going to miss out on sobriety. I was loving the beautiful opportunities, and although fearful, I was filled with excitement.

Off to England I went!. I had no idea what to expect, only that God brought me there to see if it would be a good fit for us to work together. I immediately felt the difference between our two countries. I was greeted at the airport by Karen, who planned a wonderful agenda to acquaint me with the culture. As we went to get in the car, I walked to what would be the passenger side in the States but in England is the driver's side. Of course we giggled, and she directed me to the passenger side. I put my bag in the boot (known as the trunk here in the States). As I mentioned, although the language sounded the same, it was sometimes a linguistic challenge. I was exploding inside with excitement, but my body couldn't keep up with my spirit, and I was fighting not to fall asleep from the jet lag.

As Karen and I chatted, I was captivated with the countryside and the beauty of the hills, which were blanketed in a green I'd never seen before as it contrasted against the blue of the sky. The hills were spattered with horses, goats, sheep, dogs, men and women with Wellies (boots made famous by a company called Wellington) and wax coats due to the rainy climate. That added such a richness of color. Karen's family home was nestled in a sweet countryside village called Horsted Keynes. The beautiful estate was everything you could imagine a traditional country home to look like, with beautifully appointed gardens in the back and a lovely porch. Roy and Joan (Karen's parents) welcomed me with lovely British hospitality. Joan was a spitfire who was clear about how to dwell as a guest in their home and what would be expected, although in a loving and considerate way. Roy was a handsome businessman who did quite well for himself. My room was up two flights of stairs with a landing outside. The suite was like a room in the clouds; it was heaven. I could look out my window into their incredibly beautiful backyard (which they called a garden). Oh, what a dream this was. I was so grateful and so exhausted.

The next morning, I thought, "Is this a dream? Am I really here?" I was so excited to see

EVERYTHING, I could barely contain my joy! I had coffee in the morning—it was instant, but it was wonderful. Everything tasted better in England, including Nescafé! Karen had a flat in Brighton, so she came to pick me up, and we were off. First stop was the office. As we drove out of the driveway, I was filled with excited anticipation for the unwrapping of this amazing gift. What would the drive be like? What would the office space look like? My mind was a mile a minute as we chatted and drove. The homes were made of stone, some with thatched roofs and others with slate roofs. They could not have been more perfect.

The office had once been stables that were transformed into adorable little offices. I was greeted by the beautiful and ever-loyal Pauline. She held down the fort. Anything administrative was Pauline, and if Pauline couldn't handle it, Karen could. It seemed like there was nothing Karen couldn't do. Pauline was gracious and offered to help in any way she could. She would help me get acquainted with the computer and office operation. I couldn't wait to get back to the office and set myself up. It was more than I could comprehend. Karen drove me around to get acquainted with the area. There were cute little villages with only a cemetery and a church. Haywards Heath was a little larger town, so we went shopping for some personal items I wanted to pick up. Karen took me to her favorite go-to store for "everything" in England, which became my favorite as well: Marks and Spencer. They are a combination store that has everything: groceries, a drug store, clothing, shoes, and home goods. That night, although I was still incredibly jet lagged, I found myself smiling from ear to ear with gratitude to God for such an undeserved blessing. He promised to show me amazing and unsearchable things, and my life right then was beyond my wildest dreams.

The next day we made our way to London. We took the train, and that in itself was an adventure. My enthusiasm felt palpable. We took a tour on a double-decker bus and went to Harrods and Piccadilly Square. I kept singing, "Feed the birds, tuppence a bag. Tuppence, tuppence, tuppence a bag," from Mary Poppins. To wrap up the day that I couldn't imagine could have gotten any better, we went to the London Waldorf Astoria for high tea. This is my favorite memory of all. I wore a dress I bought at Marks and Spencer the day before, beige with white polka dots, just like the one Julia Roberts wore in *Pretty Woman!* I was in awe of this grand hotel. It was like a step back in time. As we sat having English tea with a silver service, clotted cream, scones, tea sandwiches, and strawberries, I did think I had died and gone to heaven. It was divine! I remember thinking to myself, "Is this really happening, God?" I was amazed that His mercy would allow me to live out a life I could have only read about or watched on TV. I didn't feel worthy that He was so loving. I was so grateful for the gift of grace.

As I looked around, I felt like I was in 1950. Then the live trio started to play, and to my surprise, couples entered the dance floor wearing chiffon dresses that swirled as they twirled round and round. The trio was playing vintage songs that took me back to my parents' era, the 1940s and 1950s, and the older couples danced as if they were in their youth! It was as though I had stepped into a time warp. I felt the joy well up in me as I sat taking in the grandeur of the marble floors, beautiful tabletops, and gold leaf accents throughout the atrium space. When we say yes to His plans, God brings experiences to us that we couldn't possibly imagine. I wasn't sure what all of His plans for me were, but I was definitely saying yes to this dream! That night I wrote in my journal, thanking God for His mercy. I knew I didn't deserve such magnificence, but I was grateful to have it.

The days that followed consisted of traveling the countryside, visiting Mark at his home in Liverpool, meeting at the offices and going through some of the files, dinners, brainstorming . . . oh, it was exhilarating! As I travelled back to Boston, my head was filled with the plans I was going to put in place so that I could move to England. I knew everyone would be so excited for my decision, and I was too excited to be fearful. I love the spirit of spontaneity that God knitted into my soul (Philippians 4:13). As I executed my to-do list (sharing with my family, my AA friends, my cousin and her husband) things became real. Before I knew it, I had quit my job and said my goodbyes.

It says in Luke 12:32-34, *"Fear not, little flock, for it is your Father's good pleasure to give you the kingdom."* God promised His daughter the Kingdom—in my case, the United Kingdom! I couldn't believe I was really there, to live! When I first got sober, one of my counselors at rehab had said to write down what my dreams were for a year from then. Then she said that when I looked back on that year, I would realize that I sold myself short compared to the plans God had for me. Boy, if that wasn't true, I thought as I flew into Heathrow Airport prepared to move into my new life. I stayed once again at Karen's family's home in my room in the clouds, as I called it. Everything looked so beautiful, like out of a novel. I was mesmerized and realized how much of the world I had missed out on in my drunken life.

It became a ritual for me to spend time with the Lord in the morning and then go for a run. It was magical; the early morning dew and mist settled on the green pasture like the blankets on the horses while they grazed in the morning. The quiet was so still, it felt like a blanket of calm that you could almost feel the weight of. I could hear everything so clearly, like the sound of my feet, my breathing, the songbirds. I wanted more. Everything seemed brighter. The green of the grass, the flowers, the colors were so vibrant. I knew that if I was going to be successful in a new environment, then I had to be intentional with structuring my world in a new country, a new culture, and a new community. I knew if I prayed and asked God to be with me, He would, but it was still a little nerve-racking.

I learned how to drive a car on the left side of the road because I was going to be traveling a lot and they wanted me to be self-sufficient. Mark lived on the other side of London, so I didn't see him as consistently as I saw Karen. When he would come down, the three of us would brainstorm different ideas of how we could bring my American experience into the English hospitality culture. It wasn't as easy as training someone to set the table properly. It was more about being able to speak to the class structure of the United Kingdom and how it impacted the service standards and service culture in the hospitality business. We had great ideas and plans, and it was so much fun and exciting to be open to the possibility.

It didn't take me long to get accustomed to driving in England, and I loved the challenge. Now for my next adventure—my first local AA meeting. When I finally found the hall and got into my chair, I sighed a huge sigh of relief as I was surrounded by "my people." It dawned on me in the middle of the meeting that although they were English and basically spoke the same language as I did, it still was like a foreign language. I had trouble understanding them when they shared their experience, strength, and hope. They spoke very fast and used words like whilst or phrases like "at the end of the day," but through the focus of trying to understand them, I heard the language of the heart. That's the gift of an alcoholic's language. It doesn't matter what country you are in, it's still just one alcoholic helping another. My other "Aha" moment was when I realized that although I was alone in another country and across the ocean from my friends, family, and Boston AA, and although I didn't know my business partners very well or the AA people yet, they were willing to take care of me if I had any trouble. God provided the army of angels that would care for me if I had any problems. He's just like that.

The gift of desperation was alive in me, and I am so grateful for that. I knew if I wanted to stay sober in England and enjoy all that God was presenting to me, I had to keep my program first. I had a good foundation in Boston, so I did what I knew to do. I got up early and met with God in my devotions, and I journaled my journey, fears, highs, lows, and adventures. It was a myriad of feelings, excitement, fear, joy, sadness, self-doubt, and accomplishment! What I knew would keep me grounded was the safety of the twelve-step program that kept me grounded in God! I couldn't miss His marvelous presence in all that was unfolding in my life.

As my business partners and I went out looking for new business, we landed contracts with hotel companies in England, Wales, and Ireland, and we brought hospitality training and sales training to them. We coordinated events for big pharmaceutical companies and international companies that had affiliations with Boston, since my contacts were there. We traveled throughout the UK, and I was along for the ride. It was so much to take in. So many new ways of doing things: the way people did business, the way they spoke, how women were treated in business, the countryside, the language. I felt like life was in 3D, and I didn't want to miss a thing.

On one of the traveling excursions through the countryside to Wales, Mark asked if I wanted to visit a witch that did "regression." I had dabbled in palm reading and psychics, looking to be told about the Prince Charming I was waiting for to make me "truly fulfilled." Oh, those lies! At that point in my life, while I was praying to God and clinging to Him in my sobriety, I didn't truly have a relationship with Him. I had no idea about the occult or how that would be a wrong thing to dabble in. Instead, I said, "Sure, sounds fun!"

We went to a woman's home who had set up her living room as a waiting room. First Mark went into another room while I waited, and then it was my turn. I stepped into the room and lay down on a massage table. I didn't believe in regression, which is a practice that uses hypnosis to help a person remember past lives and experiences. I told the woman I didn't believe in it, but she said she thought I would be surprised.

I relaxed on the table and saw myself as a sweet, innocent, little girl of six, first grade at St. Francis de Sales Elementary School. I was in my uniform, my red hair groomed with a simple barrette. It felt so innocent, like before I started breaking the commandments, stealing my mom's M&Ms and then lying about it, or lying about getting in trouble. When I came out of the relaxed state, she asked me what I saw and what happened. After I told her, she explained her experience. She told me she couldn't get near me! She said, "You were covered with angel wings from the bottoms of your feet to the top of your head. I've never experienced anything like it." I really didn't understand how powerful the protection of God truly was at that point in my life, but I loved that it confirmed that angels were all around me. I truly didn't comprehend the danger I was playing with. It was seven years later when I truly gave my heart to the Lord that I began to comprehend God's protection in my life. Psalm 91:4 says, *"He will cover you with His feathers and under His wings you will find refuge; His faithfulness will be your shield and rampart."* A rampart is a protective structure used for defense to keep the enemies out. The Lord did that for me, even in my ignorance.

Chapter 21

BACK TO THE STATES

My life in England was nothing but wonderful as we expanded our business. I loved the time I spent with my business partners, the lessons I learned, and the beautiful hotels, castles, and people who made it feel like I was in a movie. But I knew that there would come a time when I would have to go back to the states.

When I arrived in Boston, it was an adjustment returning to life in America. The driving was now back on the side of the road I was raised with, and I couldn't go back to drinking Dunkin' Donuts coffee after the richness of French Press and the roasted coffee I had in England and other countries I had the privilege of spending time in. Now it tasted like water that had been run through a filter with used coffee grounds (sorry Dunkin' Donuts). It was wonderful to be back in the Boston AA scene, reconnecting with my friends and re-establishing relationships that were foundational to who I was in recovery. It was an exciting re-entry, but I really didn't know how to take the business from England forward. I still struggled with the same troubles with money and work ethic, and I still used chaos to avoid dealing with my own struggles.

When I left for England, my dad was diagnosed with lung cancer. He didn't want me to have any stress before leaving, so he didn't let my mother tell me what was happening. He had surgery to remove a piece of his lung while I was out of the country. After everything was said and done, they filled me in. They did not want me to come home, so they told me when my Dad got a clean bill of health after the surgery. I wrote a letter asking that they wouldn't have any more secrets. All seemed well, and he appeared to be fine until he went in for his next scan. The cancer had metastasized, and this time it was in his pancreas. Now that I was back in the States, I was going to show up and help in any way I could. The fact that I had so much going on allowed me to be so busy that I didn't have to feel.

I was traveling back home every weekend as well as trying to attract clients for the business while also helping my friend with her baking business. Chaos became a way for me to keep away the pain of my dad's diagnosis and the reality that my business was not going to become financially viable. The pie baking business was completely depleting me of my endurance because I was baking instead of sleeping in order to fulfill the orders. All my relationships were strained. As it became more and more apparent that the UK business had started to fizzle, I was not as focused on the growth of the business. Mark and Karen moved on and found another person to work in the States.

The Big Book talks about the "bedevilments" on page 52:

"(Collins Dictionary: bedevil *in American English)*

1. *to torment or harass maliciously or diabolically, as with doubts, distractions, or worries*
2. *to possess, as with a devil; bewitch*
3. *to cause confusion or doubt in; muddle; confound an issue—bedeviled by prejudices*
4. *to beset or hamper continuously*
5. *"We were having trouble with personal relationships, we couldn't control our emotional natures, we were a prey to misery and depression, we couldn't make a living, we had a feeling of uselessness, we were full of fear, we were unhappy, we couldn't seem to be of real help to other people."*

In contrast are the spiritual fruits in Galatians 5:22: *"But the fruit of the Spirit is love, joy, peace, forbearance, kindness, goodness, faithfulness, gentleness and self-control. Against such things there is no law. Those who belong to Christ Jesus have crucified the flesh with its passions and desires."* It is impossible for me to have the fruit of the Spirit if I'm not investing in my relationship with the Lord. I was so busy trying to run from my feelings, trying to appear as though I had everything under control, that I was causing more harm than good. I was hurting others with my inability to control my emotional nature. I was investing all my time into trying to look good on the outside—the international entrepreneur, the baker, the doting daughter—instead of turning to God. I was so busy trying to feel a sense of worth or value, and that kept me from feeling any emotions. The real problem was I didn't realize that I wasn't leaning into God for my support. I woke up in the morning and asked Jesus for help, I offered to do His will, I read my devotionals, I went to meetings, I was helping my family. How could I not be in a relationship with Him?

In my opinion, self-reliance is one of the devil's greatest tools. Just because I thought I was "working a good program" doesn't mean I was. My motivation for everything I did was laden in dishonesty: I wanted what I wanted the way I wanted when I wanted it! I was motivated by actions that would make me look good. I would tell a ridiculous story so you wouldn't know that I made a mistake or when I didn't know the answer or what to do. It was all about how I looked. Full stop.

The disease of alcoholism is funny. After you put down the drink, it's no longer the drinking that's the problem; it's the thinking. Alcoholics who have surrendered to the disease don't realize that no longer drinking is not going to be enough to succeed in life. At least it wasn't enough for me. I'm a "Real Alcoholic," and I tried rationalizing and justifying why I wasn't giving my all and working as hard as I should have to launch this new business in the States. I loved to talk about how I lived in England and was heading up North

America Operations. It sounded so important. When it came down to making the phone calls and putting in the work, I was all over the place. I tried to rationalize and justify my wrongful behavior, and I was too distracted from all that I was filling my God-size hole with to ask God for the help I needed. God knew the truth, and in His mercy, He let me carry on without completely crushing me.

Chapter 22

DADDY'S LITTLE GIRL

As my dad's disease progressed, hospice was introduced into his care. It was a great blessing to my mother, but there was no question where I needed to be. I moved to Amsterdam, New York, where my parents had retired, fully understanding that in a very small town in Upstate New York, the AA meetings were going to be limited. I knew I was going to need to find something to do while I was caring for my father and helping my mom.

If you remember, towards the end of my drinking, I tried to join the Air Force because I wanted to fly airplanes. One day while I was out running errands, I went through a little town called Schoharie off Route 5, and I noticed a little grass strip airfield that used to be used by General Electric. They offered flight lessons. Once again, when I least expected a blessing, God provided a way to materialize the whispers of my heart, right when I needed it the most. I began to learn to fly in a little Cessna 152.

The thing I find amazing about God blessing us with the "whispers of our heart" is that it is never about just the surface desire; it's the blessing that's deep below it. God not only blessed me with my heart's desire, He had a deeper blessing—the true blessing of my life—which was the healing of my relationship with my father. That is how God works! He always goes beyond all we can hope or imagine; all we have to do is say yes to His promptings!

My father was one of three boys, and he had three boys before I came along. Quite honestly, he didn't know what to do with me. He loved me for sure, but when I thought of my dad, I really didn't know him. Sure, I knew the superficial stories of his life, but it took me time after he passed for me to understand the remarkable man that he really was. I always wanted my dad to tell me I was his "little girl." I was his only girl, so why would he have to say that? I knew he was in World War II and loaded bombs in the South Pacific, but what I didn't know was that his desire was to be a pilot, just like mine was. He got an Airplane Mechanics license because the young men who became pilots were flying into Japan and a large percentage weren't flying out. So when I started flying, we had a whole new world of conversation open to us. It was so much more than I could have ever hoped for in just achieving my pilot's license. I received a heart connection with my dad. We would talk for hours after my lessons, and he would ask me questions about the plane, go through the pre-flight checklist, talk about rudders and flaps and fuselage. Through this connection, I became the person he could talk to regarding dying and how he wanted to go with dignity. It was so hard on my mother letting go of her love of a lifetime; watching him suffer was a burden that he didn't want to put on her, and yet, there was nothing he could do about it.

Hospice is a wonderful organization. They not only care for patients physically with every possible need for the deterioration of the body, but they meet the patient spiritually to prepare for meeting Jesus. I love that they follow your lead; they are not there to evangelize, just to love! They will ask their patients questions that will prepare them for the end of life. Your choice is between you and God, and they respect that! My dad felt comfortable sharing with me how frustrated he was that he could no longer eat anything or enjoy a drink, that he just was "existing." He was always a strong man and never sick. I don't think I can ever recall my dad calling out sick. Never. He was strong and resourceful, but the cancer made him weak and dependent. This was 1995, and the American pathologist and euthanasia proponent, Murad Jacob Kevorkian, was controversially championing a terminal patient's right to die. I guess we can't understand what we don't know. My father's life was over, in his opinion, because he couldn't enjoy anything that made his life worth living. He was in constant, excruciating pain, but he had a strong body, so he just had to wait for it to wear out. The diagnosis of pancreatic cancer is generally a three to six month life expectancy, at most. My dad lasted about ten months.

The Shootist was John Wayne's last movie; he died three years later to cancer, just like in the film. I watched it with my dad one night. In the story, the gunfighter is aging and has cancer. The beauty of the movie was the dignity that the gunfighter was able to end his life with. My dad wanted to end his life with dignity, and my mom and I worked very hard to provide him with that, but the deterioration of a body is not a journey for the faint of heart, and you truly are in a state of powerlessness. For my dad, that was the hardest part.

He said to me that night, "See, Honey, that's how I wish I could go."

I just hugged him and said, "I know, Daddy. I'm sorry you have to suffer."

He passed a few weeks after that. I'm grateful my flying gave him something to think about other than his plight. Three days before he passed, he asked me, "Did you go up, honey?" I said no, we have a few things going on here. He said, "Don't stop flying, or you won't get back to it." I promised I wouldn't, and I didn't, for as long as I could.

After Dad passed, I knew I couldn't stay in Amsterdam, New York! All the business (or busynesses) that I was involved with had all gone on to whatever they were to become. I had been in a precious bubble that surrounded me with safety and security. Walking someone to heaven's door puts everything into laser-focus. I went back to the Boston area, and although I didn't know what to do, I knew one thing—I wanted to keep flying! My friend Hallie and her wonderful mother helped me with living accommodations on Cape Cod. I was so grateful to have the privilege of living that winter in Hyannisport, Massachusetts. As I traveled back and forth to Boston, I noticed an airport sign that led me to a small airfield by Norwood Memorial Airport in Norwood, Massachusetts. One day I found the courage to go in. I told them my story about flying while my dad was in hospice and explained how I wanted to keep flying. I didn't have the money, but I was willing to work for flight time. I was willing to clean planes, clean the office, anything they needed. I would do anything they needed in exchange for flight time. The owner looked at me pensively, as if he was summing it all up. He liked my "chutzpah," and said he would let me work as a dispatcher for the pilots that departed from our FBO and his Flight School. Oh, I was ecstatic! He could only pay me a stipend, but he would set me up to learn from his best instructor, his partner George. George was a boisterous, no-holds-barred kind of guy, but a real teddy bear once you got to know him. I couldn't wait to get started. There were still many details that were not in place, but this was my heart's desire, and God always materializes the whispers of the heart in His way and His timing.

I had so much fun exploring the world of aviation. My job consisted of coordinating the schedule for the instructors, greeting the pilots in training, keeping the office looking presentable, and generally providing a welcoming environment. It was such a blessing to be part of this world. Eventually, it was time for my solo flight. I prepared my flight plan, and George reviewed it. I performed the flight check list: all clear. I looked around and knew that this was a moment in my life I would never forget. It was one of those beautiful, calm, clear mornings, and I was so nervous. As I taxied to the runway, my heart was racing! I was confident in knowing that I was prepared, however it was just me in the pilot seat getting ready for takeoff.

"Piper Warrior Niner 333 Alpha Oscar, ready for takeoff."

Full throttle and lift—oh, that feeling when the wheels are off the ground, and it's just you and the air! As I climbed higher and higher, I looked over to the jump seat, and my eyes were flooded with tears. I knew my dad was with me for that flight, filled with pride and loving that his little girl materialized his dream and that we shared heaven in that moment. I love you, Daddy!

Chapter 23

AWAKENING

My mom really wanted to help me get on my feet. She was so grateful for our time as we cared for my dad. It made it so much easier for her to have me around to lighten the atmosphere while we gardened, cooked, and laughed. It was a difficult season, and I'm so grateful to God that I was sober and able to be the daughter they deserved. Serving my mom and dad through such a vulnerable season felt especially right since I had caused so much pain for so many years! I believe and have experienced "living amends," a tool that allows God to work through you to bless others. Through this action, He graciously blesses you with healing through building your self-esteem. Only a loving God can repair so compassionately.

I had learned and experienced so much in England, like my ability to negotiate, my desire to make an event a memory, my experience in the hotel industry, sales training, and ability to put that all together to create a business. I decided to start an event planning business. We named it SQI, Shannon (my grandmother's maiden name) Q (for my maiden name Quist) International! I got a studio apartment in Cambridge, Massachusetts, and set up shop. The landlord was cute, but I was going to stay focused on the building of my business. My dear friend Dodi worked at American

Express Travel with big corporate clients. When I told her I was starting an event planning business, she said she had a contact at a big-name corporation whose events were too small for the American Express event planning department. Just like that, I landed Motorola. I needed help, so I asked my friend Jim and his cousin Mary. My weakness was always finance—pricing, asking for money up front, things like that. I didn't manage the finances well. But we did manage.

Life was moving at a fast pace. I ended up dating the landlord. His name was George, and he was very handsome. I knew he liked me, but there was one problem. We were polar opposites in our beliefs. I wanted to raise children with the foundation of a relationship with God, and he was an atheist. I convinced myself (there's that self-sufficiency again) that it would be fine, that having different philosophies would be a balanced way to allow the children to see both sides of the spectrum. The truth of the matter was simple. I wanted someone to take care of me, and I was willing to abandon my Godly beliefs for it. This awareness did not come quickly; I had to go through a painful, albeit necessary, process. God put me on a journey to reveal the truth of my willful ways. God wanted a relationship with me. I had faith after my experience with my brother, getting sober, remembering how He kept me alive, and the miracles of how I "came to" just before I hit the guardrails. I couldn't miss His presence in my life, and yet, there I was, willing to give up the one thing that sustained me all my life for a used car and a house that was his, not mine. It took me some time to see the distorted justification, but God always has a way of working the truth out, especially when we are clueless. He is so merciful!

My first "Aha" moment was when we were on a walk, and he was talking about one of his close friends. He shared that he was having an affair.

I said, "Did you talk to him about how he should end it and make it right with his wife?"

He said, "Why would I do that? If he is happy, then I don't see any harm."

I thought, "Did I just hear, 'As long as he was happy?'" WOW, how did he not comprehend that the deeper meaning of his friend's actions was deception and betrayal? I couldn't escape that we were not on the same page for a lot of life decisions, but I remained in my delusion. The dilemma was that if I accepted that this man wasn't for me, then I had failed again. The signs were neon, but I was tired of not having enough. I was thirty-seven, and I wanted a man who could provide the security of a nice house (check), a new car (it was used, but it had AC, which was a huge step up, check), adventure (sailing on his catamaran, check), someone to provide for me (with conditions . . . check). I knew that if I made the decision to marry him, I would be taken care of. I just couldn't escape the nagging feeling that I would probably not be married to a "best friend." My willful nature said, "We will deal with that later."

How many times have we heard that beauty will always flow out of our pain? God always meets me where I am, and if it's uncomfortable, and I want to run away, He has me stay in the discomfort so He can show me what the REAL PROBLEM IS!

Well, boy did I get a teaching!

I loved my work. We were doing events all over the world. Quebec City, Florida, Portugal, San Diego. I did site visits in Helsinki, Puerto Rico, and St. Kits. We also did small training groups in the Mansfield area. There were only three of us, and the workload was heavy. It was my business, so I assumed the responsibility of staying as long as I needed to meet the needs of my clients. It was such an exciting time. I was still going to AA because I knew I still needed that support of community, especially as my romantic relationship was challenging. My six-year anniversary in AA was upon me, and as anyone could see, I had it all! So why was I feeling so empty inside? Why was I still lying about why I was late for a business that I owned? Why couldn't I manage my money and constantly had to rob from Peter to pay Paul?

I celebrated my six-year milestone by sharing my story at the AA meeting I went to on Saturdays. It was my Home Group, and I never missed it unless I was traveling. A Home Group is the group you are committed to showing up to every week. You have a service position in that group, and you get to know the people who attend that group well, and they get to know you. It's a level playing field; we all came back from the gates of hell by God's grace, and although the circumstances are different, the feelings are the same. As you share your highs and lows of life, you have the privilege of following along with each other's journey. You celebrate the successes, and you share in the pain. You make time for each other. The community becomes like family.

When it's your anniversary, you have the honor and privilege of sharing your story. As I was sharing about all the blessings of my "fabulous life," I started to cry. They say if you want to hear God, take a shower . . . or you could share your story in an AA meeting on your sixth anniversary. It was at that moment I recognized that I was miserable. I had everything on the outside that would make me happy—a car with air conditioning, the president of my own company, international travel, engaged to a great guy, future financial security. All the material things. However, I was restless, irritable, and discontent. It was the deep, important matters that were missing from the depth of my soul, the secrets I was keeping from myself, let alone everyone else. That was what kept me separated from God and my fellows. I could look like I had it all, but it was a facade. My business looked like it was flourishing, but it had no financial cushion. We were floating from event to event. My fiancé had no interest in growing with me in my spiritual walk by growing closer to God. It was like there was no place inside myself to push down the lies I needed to tell others and myself. All this came to me as I was sharing how wonderful my life was at this Saturday morning AA meeting.

God is so gracious with me, though. He will always provide a solution when I'm ready to surrender to the next level of my powerlessness. This time He did it through the example of witnessing a miraculous change in a friend of mine. Her name is Nancy. She was beautiful, funny, witty, eloquent, and angry. But as time went by through the year, I watched her change. She used to share how she would overreact with her daughter and husband. On that Saturday, she shared how her little girl dropped a drawer in the kitchen, and when Nancy came over to help her clean up, her little girl looked up at her with tears in her eyes, and said, "You're not going to yell at me, Momma?" Nancy started to cry. She explained that working the steps had changed her as God was now doing for her what she could not do herself.

After the meeting, Nancy talked with me. I said, "I don't know what you are doing, but I have watched you change, and I need to change. I got sober to live happy, joyous, and free, but right now, if this is as good as it gets, I might as well drink or end my life." I had reached another bottom, but this time I was SOBER! It's one thing to get sober and realize you have caused harm, lived dishonestly, and created chaos while you were drinking, but to live with the same behavior without the anesthesia of alcohol or drugs takes you to a whole other level of desperation.

Alcohol is but a symptom. I had been on a wild ride those past six years, from new hotel, to England, to pie business, to Dad's cancer, to flying planes, to NOW. Self Will Run Riot. Although I believed in God, did my morning devotionals, said my prayers, went to meetings, asked for direction, turned my will and my life over to the care of God, my relationship with God was in my intentions, NOT my actions. I was dishonest with my actions. I would present what I felt needed to be heard as an acceptable response, but it was generally laced in lies of omission so I could look the way I needed people to see me and not the cold reality of how I was truly living. Although I was running a company, alcoholism was still alive and well, and it wasn't getting treated because "I was *sooo* busy and important." The thought of drinking wasn't the problem, my thinking was the problem. I was still engaged in alcoholic behavior.

What does that mean exactly? Well, in addition to not being able to see the true from the false and lying about even the slightest details to protect the image, there was unreasonable anger. If someone wasn't doing what I wanted them to do, the way I wanted them to do it, I would react in anger and frustration. Financially, I was robbing Peter to pay Paul (George would bail me out when I was running short). I was presenting as though I was successful in the business when I could barely keep the lights on. I appeared to have it all together, when in reality, I had no financial strategy or financial sense. I just knew how to work hard.

I asked Nancy's sponsor to sponsor me. I jumped in, desperate to change. I was willing to do whatever was suggested, and there were a lot of suggestions. Just like at the end of my drinking, I didn't know how to live without alcohol as a crutch, now I had to learn how to live life without the crutch of dishonesty and self-reliance, my old ways of coping.

As I worked with my sponsor, I saw that I completely understood that first part of the First Step (admit I was powerless over alcohol). I was an alcoholic, I had no question about that, but the second part of the First Step (that my life was unmanageable), I never really processed before. Boy, was it unmanageable. The best I could do was to achieve all the outside things and still feel like I was a fraud and unable to manage my finances. My self-centered fear ruled my thoughts, making me feel like my friends and family thought less of me. I had spent all those years in sobriety just waiting for everything to change because I wasn't drinking any longer. Wasn't that enough? The simple answer to that question was, NO.

I had done just enough in my recovery to stay sober. I was desperate to do what I was told when I first came into AA, and all my energy was focused on staying away from a drink. My behavior was still dishonest; I was lying about my character defects. A perfect example was when my employee asked why I was late, I would make up a story instead of just admitting I got tied up getting out of the house. Afterward I would go into my office and think, "Why did I feel as though I had to lie? It's my business. It doesn't matter why I was late." As I unfolded the second part of the First Step, as well as the Second Step, "Came to believe in a power greater than myself," I saw the insanity of going to any length to look good.

The power of working through the Twelve Steps out of the Big Book of *Alcoholics Anonymous* is transformative. The main ingredient is a willingness to look at every nook and cranny of your life. It will reveal the root of your pain, which is that you are powerless, and the solution, which is power. In *Alcoholics Anonymous*, it states, "The ego must be smashed." This is not the boastful ego that screams how great we are, it is the quiet ego that is self-reliant, insanely believing that we know what's best for our life when clearly it hasn't worked over and over again.

Humility can only be accessed by telling someone what your plan is, then listening. This was the only way I could sort out my old way of doing things, which had been taking action without asking for direction, and then begging for forgiveness. I was amazed at the results. God met me every time, but taking the right action looked like having to tell the truth at all costs. When I did lie, I had to go back and tell the person that I lied. It surprised me to see how willful I really was. I would call my sponsor with all sorts of scenarios, always so sure she was going to see it my way, and it never ceased to amaze me when she would call me out on seeing the truth and taking the right action. Every time I did, God met me with the peace and freedom from the obsessive thoughts as I rationalized and justified my behavior over and over again or tried to ignore the right action as if it was going to just go away, and I could try it again another time. That was my modus operandi: "I'll do the right thing the next time, Lord. I can't take the right action right now because the right action would have me call out my wrongful behavior, and I would either not get what I wanted or I would look like a mess-up." That kept me in a state of perpetual fear, until I took my Third Step (Made a decision to turn our will and our lives over to the care of God, as we understood Him) and prayed the prayer with understanding: "God, I offer myself to Thee to build with me and to do with me all Thy wilt. Relieve me of the bondage of self that I may better do Thy will. Take away the difficulties that victory over them may bear witness to You and my fellows. May I do Thy will always." I then was able to be desperately willing to expose the lies in my head to someone and ask for help in taking the next right action, no matter how uncomfortable it would be.

Making that decision was where I found breakthrough. God couldn't work on me if I wasn't willing to do something different. Telling the truth about what was in my head was the action. As I entered into the Fourth Step (Made a searching and fearless moral inventory of myself), it took time to weed through the rationalizing I had spent a lifetime building up as my tool for navigation, my delusional approach to life. Okay, what does "delusional approach to life" really mean? Well, it means that I have a play going on in my head about how life should be, and how you, as the actors in my play, are supposed to act. When I think that you are supposed to answer me a certain way or accommodate me a certain way, and you don't, I react based on self-centered fear, usually defensively. This causes a chain of uncomfortable behavior that never needed to take place if I had just recognized that it wasn't about me. If I could have accepted the person's response without thinking about myself, then I wouldn't have had a reaction, and all would be well.

I could not get this clear way of thinking without talking with someone, in my case a sponsor. But it doesn't have to stop with AA. Let's say you are a person who goes to church to find peace. Ask one of the leaders to help you find a mentor who can help you spiritually navigate your life. A sick mind can't fix a sick mind. Bible studies are another great way to discuss the struggles you may have, but you have to be willing to be honest about how you live life. For me, only God could help me excavate my true self, and it had to start with the desperate desire to live life differently! To live as He designed life to be so I could exist in peace and love instead of chaos and discord. It was humbling to ask for help in the most basic life skills like spending money, or question if I had to tell the truth about a situation. My life was surrounded by my dishonest behavior, and it took intention to be willing to get "cash register" honest. What that means is, I had to be completely transparent with my thinking and behavior so I could receive an honest appraisal of my perception of the situation.

This journey of the Fourth Step took much longer than I had ever expected. I was "very busy." My experience shows me that when I have something that is going to be hard emotionally, I tend to get busy doing other things. I knew this Fourth Step was going to provide freedom, but I was "very busy" and "important" with my business. My events were all-consuming, and my boyfriend clearly needed my direction in life if he was going to become the man of my dreams. When was I going to have time to write out each resentment for each person? (And I mean each person.)

I was thirty-seven years old, and I was still resentful of the little blonde in second grade who got the role of Gretl in *The Sound of Music*. The decision was simply, "She looked the part," and I was the awkward redhead. I wrote the inventory of resentment when I could, and sometimes that was on planes when traveling for an event. One time I was writing my Fourth Step on a plane coming back from a site visit. When I got off the plane and got home, I realized I lost the whole first part of my inventory. I was frantic! I called the airlines and went to the lost and found at Logan International, but there was no notebook. I'm sure it got thrown out. Oh my, what will I do? I had no choice but to start again, and I knew it was for a reason. I wasn't going to quit; I needed to get freedom, and the only way that was going to happen was to finish. I started the process over again from the list I had created, and God, as He always does, blessed me with clarity and precision as to my actions.

A perfect example of my self-righteous anger during this process was with my brother Charles. He and I had a strained relationship. I judged him with distortion and bitterness. I was traveling to my mother's to go to a wedding of a dear family friend, and I had just found out that Charles was moving in with my mother to go back to school for nursing and get his Masters as well as work in the Albany area. I was driving on the Mass Turnpike and thought I should call my sponsor and talk to her about what I was going to tell him, that he had no business moving home as he was going to cause chaos for my mother. My sponsor listened for about five to ten minutes and then suggested I pull over. She asked if my mother had asked me if it was a good idea to have my brother move in with her. I said, no. She then told me it really was none of my business. I reluctantly agreed. She proposed that I do the following: pray to see how I am JUST LIKE HIM (well, that sent me into a tailspin, as I was the one in recovery, and I am NOTHING like him), stop before I go into the house and pray that God would show me how I could be of service to him, and then not talk about myself but only inquire about his life and how he is doing.

Wow. I did not expect those suggestions, but I did them. I ranted the rest of the way to New York and cried out, "I'm the one who is doing the right things now!" The Lord just kept quietly reminding me that anger is not His way, and that if I wanted freedom, I needed to try what my mentor suggested. When I turned onto my mother's street, I pulled the car over and asked God to show me how I am like my brother and to help me be willing to be kind and of service. When I pulled in the driveway, my brother met me to bring my bags up to my room. My mom and I gathered in the kitchen, and he joined. When my mom went to bed, I sat out on the porch with my brother and asked him about his journey and what he thought about this new chapter in his life. It was a lovely evening and a healing weekend. If I hadn't been willing to take that suggestion and leave my ego with God, I would not have the blessing of my brother's friendship. He is such a gift to my life. It wasn't his behavior that was the problem, it was my perception of who he was. All the times I have been willing to take the opposite action to my self-righteous delusion, God meets me every time.

When I finally finished my Fourth Step, I went to my sponsors and spent the weekend. It was obviously a LONG inventory, and before we started reading my Fifth Step (Admitted to God, myself, and another human being the exact nature of our wrongs) to my sponsor, we invited God into the process so He could reveal the problem, which was my self-reliance, and the solution, which is His power. The incredible relief of realizing that my shameful behavior that was saturated in self-hate was the result of my alcoholism, and that it was the best I could do without including God into my life and relationships.

At the end of the weekend, I saw over and over that it didn't matter who the person was that I was resentful toward, my self-seeking actions were repeated due to my selfish thinking and delusional conclusion of what I believed others were doing or thinking. I always ended up with the same dysfunctional results. The patterns of my behavior were clearly laid out by reading the Fourth Step. I saw that I was repeating the same ugly behavior, just with a different person in a different place and time. I was so ready to have that removed. As a result of this realization, I had hope, armed with the truth of why I did the things I did, and I knew that I could live differently. For the first time, I really understood that "selfishness and self-centeredness were the root of the trouble, driven by a hundred forms of fear, self-delusion, self-seeking, and self-pity, I stepped on the toes of my fellows, and they retaliated. Seemingly without provocation, but we invariably find, that sometime in the past we have made decisions based on self which later put us in the position to be hurt" (*Alcoholics Anonymous, page 62*).

I was now ready for Step Six (We became willing to ask God to help us remove our defects of character). The suggestion is to review the first five principles (steps) to make sure you were thorough and held nothing back. After you have done this in meditation, envision yourself walking through the arch (created by the foundation of the first step, the cornerstone of the second step, and the keystone of the third step) a free man, in my case a free woman! I don't think I had ever experienced so much peace and sense of accomplishment for actually finishing what I set out to do, but more work was required. Action!

After I walked through the arch and was willing to have God remove my defects of character, I had to ask Him to remove them. I prayed the prayer in Step Seven on page 76 (Humbly ask Him to remove our shortcomings).

> *My Creator, I am now willing that you should have all of me, good and bad. I pray that you now remove from me every single defect of character that stands in the way of my usefulness to you and my fellows. Grant me strength as I go out from here to do your bidding. Amen.*

The reason we don't put an "Amen" at the end of the Third Step and we do at the Seventh is because the Third Step is the process of offering ourselves to be willing to have God show us the truth no matter how much it will hurt. The Fourth, Fifth, and Sixth Steps are the process of realization and purging of the old ways. God's action through our willingness to be obedient rewards us with a peace that surpasses all knowledge and understanding. After we humbly ask Him to remove the shortcomings, now we can say "Amen." Through this, we become a vessel for Him to use as He needs. Amen means "we agree."

The Eighth Step (Made a list of all persons we had harmed and became willing to make amends to them all) is a list that we take from our Fourth Step which prepares us to do our Ninth Step (Made direct amends to such people wherever possible, except to do so would injure them or others). Much discussion in the recovery world is focused on the Fourth Step, and understandably so, but my experience was that the Ninth Step developed my trust in God. Either He was everything, or He was nothing; either He is or He isn't. What was my choice to be? This is where people struggle to finish the journey of recovery. It is one thing to admit your struggles to God and another human being, but now you are expected to go to a person and tell them how wrong you were? Isn't that a little much? Can't we just let sleeping dogs lie? As I determined in my Sixth Step, I was willing, but the Ninth Step takes a faith and trust in God that He will catch me when I fall. I just knew I would be judged and discarded when I admitted my harmful behavior. But I was blessed with the Gift of Desperation. I wanted to be transformed, and I knew that meant I had to be willing to face those that I had harmed. They say it gets worse before it gets better, and that was my experience.

I wrote out my amends with my sponsor and edited and edited as I struggled with being vague about my behavior. It was a process to take my self-seeking behavior and clearly spell out what I had done. The process of having the paper or card to read the amend was most helpful as it kept me on point. I would get the go-ahead from my sponsor, and then came actually making the call. This was back in the early 90s when we still had home phones. I would get on my knees and make the call to schedule the appointments. I had financial amends to hotels that were no longer owned by the same company. I sat in the office of a new Director of Human Resources who had just started the job. I thought I owed the company

$2000 from when I left for England. I scheduled the appointment, showed up, and asked if I could read the letter. I had made personal long-distance phone calls from my office; I barely gave a full day of work; I used the expense account for personal items; and I left the company even though I thought I had an outstanding bill. The Director of Human Resources looked at me when I was finished as I dried my tears, and he said, "I'm not much of a spiritual man, but you have just restored my faith in humanity. This industry is riddled with this kind of behavior, but I have never experienced anyone who was accountable and had enough courage to call it out." He also said that he looked through my file and found nothing regarding any outstanding bill. He thanked me for coming in. That's how God operates. He blesses others with restoration they didn't even know they needed. He blessed me with a financial miracle; I had nothing at the time.

God met me in that very powerful way with every amend I was to make. The biggest at the time was with George. I knew he was not the man for me. I could have married him and just accepted that we were not going to meet on a spiritual plane. But I believed in my soul that God did not want me to settle, so I had to accept the fact that I was thirty-eight, and this would probably be my last shot at getting married.

I had planned a trip out to visit my cousin Grace in California. I was excited to fill her in on all the details of my engagement. Of course we were thrilled to see each other. It was at dinner that she told me she couldn't get excited about me marrying George. She thought he was not the right one for me. I don't think I ever was so angry, especially with Grace. I always counted on her to support me in my decisions, so I was taken aback when she did not express excitement or support. My friend Jeffrey lived in San Francisco; I needed some space to process all this. I called Jeffrey (who I had always had a crush on since the first day I laid eyes on him in the Boston AA meeting) and asked him to come and pick me up. He said he'd be right down, and we went to San Francisco to spend the day.

Jeffrey and I got sober together. He came into AA a year before I did. We went to the same meetings and became friends over time. I shared my experiences in the meetings: job changes, moving to England, my father's pancreatic cancer, my business. His dad was diagnosed with a brain tumor, and I was able to be his "go-to" since I had walked the journey he was now embarking on. We had become close friends. He showed me his cool apartment in Nob Hill. We went to a meeting at the Dry Dock which was an AA Clubhouse in San Francisco. It was a wonderful day. As I talked about my frustration with Grace, his reply was not what I had expected. He said, "Well, Red (that is what he called me), you would think that if you're marrying the guy, you would be in agreement about at least ONE of the major life decisions." OUCHH.

When I got back to my cousin's house, she said, "I don't get it. Jeff is wonderful, cute and you light up when you see him. Why aren't you with him?"

That trip actually confirmed what I already knew to be true, that I was not going to marry George. Now it was only a matter of time before I would make my amends to him. I had to write the amends which would bring the truth of my selfish behavior to the forefront. I could no longer make my unhappiness about George. I had to take accountability for my dishonesty in entering into a relationship with him. Then it seemed like the flood gates of all the wrongful behavior came to mind. I was so grateful that I was on this journey of recovery so I would be able to acknowledge that my choices, without God, caused harm to innocent people because they were never supposed to be a part of the story. It gave me the insight of how I dishonestly entered into this relationship hoping that he would take care of me financially. I ignored all the warning signs and moved through the relationship, rationalizing my behavior and blaming him for his. I was able to see that when I didn't get what I demanded, I punished him (or any other person) through silent scorn, blaming, and gossiping. When I finished my amends with George, he thanked me for my honesty and thoroughness. He said, although he loved me, he deserved to have someone who would love him for who he was, not who they wanted him to be. I left him well. God is so good! But now—the cleanup. All moved out with no place to go!

Chapter 24

FROM SINGLE TO SACRED

My business was closing. Motorola put a freeze on events and travel, and from there, all that I had built on my own self-reliance began to crumble because of my selfish, dishonest ways. I struggled with being able to build the business, so we were just existing to support the business we had, and not well at all. Now that George wasn't covering me from check to check, I had no savings to keep us afloat. My dishonest approach to managing money and selfishly overextending myself and the business caused me to harm my employees. As I got more honest with my harmful behavior, I knew what I had to do, but with every fiber of my being, I did not want to have to speak the words. "Oh, Lord, what will they think? They will hate me. I can't! Only you can bless me with the courage to make this possible." I knew I had to make amends with them, but that meant that I also had to be honest and say I didn't have any more money. Period. No insurance, no last paycheck, at least for now. The reality was I had to let go of my employees. I did them such a terrible disservice. It was a horrible conversation that left them angry and disappointed, and rightfully so. I knew a more thorough amend was due to them, but the honest truth and clarity of my selfish, dishonest behavior was all that could be communicated at the time. I couldn't possibly feel the emotion of the harmful impact I made on the two of them. This was probably the hardest amends I had to make do to the fact it was one of my worst harms. Now I had to orchestrate the next job before me—to finish the last event on the books, find a place to live, and find work.

Because this was such a heavy burden to carry, I did feel a sense of relief, and as I made more and more amends, God met me and blessed me with a freedom from the mental obsession of the loud noise. More action of living out the amends required more discomfort, but it was so necessary.

I needed a place to stay, and my dearest friend invited me to live with her and her sister. This move was temporary, of course, and under the advisement of my sponsor, I gave a time limit that I would stay. I continued to make amends, but if I was going to have to find a place to stay, I would need money. I was in the middle of planning my last event for Motorola in Portugal. I had to let go of my offices because I didn't have the money for them, and I had to make the call to the IRS to inquire what I could do to pay off the debt when I could only pay a small sum every month. God met me with grace and mercy every single step of the way. As I packed up the offices, my time was coming to a close for the place where I was staying. What was I to do? My friend allowed me to put my things in her garage for storage. I had a month, and when that was up, my sponsor talked to me about the selfishness of taking advantage of others' generosity with their time and sacrifice. There would be no extended stay. When I had made a commitment to a set amount of time, I was to honor that and not allow my discomfort to become a burden to my friendship. My word was my word, yes meant yes, and no meant no. I couldn't take advantage of my friendship as I made a commitment of time, and my living there put a strain on her and her sister's relationship.

I stayed in the office for the last nights before moving out of there, and now I was truly just relying on God. I had nothing. NO money, NO place to live, NO income that could be used for my comfort. I had to trust Him and continue to take the action of moving forward. My next step in my free fall was to find a simple room while I waited to finish this last event. The options were slim. I didn't have enough money to get an apartment yet. But seriously? The only thing I could afford was the YWCA! I humbly went to the office of the YWCA and registered for the week. It was clean, simple, and I was grateful to have a place to stay. I had to be willing to go to any lengths. Humility is such a powerful experience. It's a posture of knowing that, of and by yourself, you have nothing except for the "knowing" that God will provide.

At this point, I couldn't miss it. Cleaning up my wreckage left me with literally nothing. I looked at it as a clean slate, a "do over," an opportunity to become the person God designed me to be. To become that, it meant letting go of my old tools, my old ideas, now that the noise of the mental obsession had quieted because I was walking in integrity. Grace and dignity can't be present without integrity. Honestly, I was excited with the anticipation of what might unfold. What did God have in store?

I desperately needed cash, but I had to execute this last beautiful event in Portugal. My friend Nancy's husband was one of the corporate chefs at Legal Sea Food's Corporate Kitchen, and he arranged for an interview with their Chestnut Hill Restaurant. They hired me to be a food runner. Humility followed me (have you picked up that I had a big ego?). I certainly was over-qualified, but I needed the cash. I didn't have to clock in until 6:00 PM, and I could leave when it slowed down. There was a collection of tips, and then the servers would tip you out. I was so, so grateful.

As it happened, a new General Manager started the same night I did. Actually, he was not just your average General Manager. He was working on a corporate merger with Massport. They were the Massachusetts Transportation Department for Boston Logan, the Public Transportation and Water Transportation, taking over one of their facilities (see God's divine orchestration) and Legal Sea Foods. He brought together Roger Berkowitz, the President and CEO of Legal Sea Foods, and Peter Blume, the President of Massport, to take over the Boston Fish Auction Center which was renovated and turned into Massport's Executive Conference Center.

When he saw I was running food, he called me into his office and said, "What are you doing?

Why are you in this position?" I explained my circumstances and that I just needed to make money until I could finish my event in Portugal. He asked about my experience in the hospitality industry, and I explained how I started in hotels and worked my way into corporate sales, my partnership with event planning and sales training, all the way up to my most present job as the president of an event company with Motorola as my primary client. He was very complimentary and explained that they were procuring the Exchange Conference Center on the Boston Fish Pier and needed to present a marketing plan to the Board of Legal Sea Foods as to why and how this could be successful. Since I had a lot of experience in the Boston Corporate Market because I had opened the ITT Sheraton Conference Center, I was pretty confident I could put together a marketing plan, and so I did. My first night as a humble food runner, God rewarded me with a beautiful plan that showed me my next path.

> *"Trust in the Lord with all your*
> *heart, and do not lean on your own*
> *understanding. In all your ways*
> *acknowledge him and He will make*
> *straight your path."*
> Proverbs 3:5-6

During the week I was staying at the Y, a friend of mine had a friend who needed a house sitter. It was last minute and was the exact dates that took me up to the Portugal event. Again, God provided me with a beautiful condo, in Jamaica

Plain, right on Jamaica Pond. I was able to finish the final details in an environment that was clean, beautiful, and provided a bit of nature to ease my anxious spirit. All the T's were crossed and the I's dotted, I was ready to go. I knew the job before me was going to be long hours and hard on my body, but I had such a lightness of spirit and a hope for the future. God made it so I wouldn't have to worry during the event; I would be able to focus on my guests and take care of my client! I finished my house sitting, and off I went. I was flying TAP Portugal out of Boston Logan. What a wonderful experience. And the coffee . . . oh my gosh, so rich. I have no idea how they made it, but oh my goodness. I still think about it all these years later.

My job was done, and it was a success. The event came off without a hitch, the attendees couldn't have been happier with the accommodations and the off-property events, and God once again gave me the gift of closing a season well! I was all excited for my next new adventure!

Upon my return, I was eager to hear how the board meeting went with Legal Sea Foods. They loved the idea, and I was hired in marketing with a salary and health insurance working for the premiere restaurant chain in New England to expand the business into Corporate Catering. God's plans are always better than I could have ever imagined. I mean, all I did was show up willing to humble myself, and God blessed me mightily!!

When I got back from Portugal, I had to look immediately for a place to live. I found a little studio apartment in Waltham, Massachusetts. The owner of the house was a kind man who allowed me to move in right away. It was truly the gift of God's grace as the details just fell into place. A studio to live in, a new job with lots of potential, and a whole new beginning. God is so good to me.

I started the job and absolutely loved it! We were building a whole new division to the restaurant chain, and I was a part of all of it. Not only was the job exciting, but I felt God was building a new life for me as I was transformed by God through the steps. I felt taken care of as I lived out each day honestly and humbly. This was what it was like living authentically and in God's will. I felt His presence as I walked through my days and had the feel of His touch as I would see His hand in the details. I started to run again and joined the L Street Running Club in South Boston. I finally understood what "running high" was all about as I ran farther distances.

Since I was going to be thirty-nine, I decided to close out the thirty decade with a bucket list item: run the Boston Marathon! So, I started training for it. My life consisted of work, meetings, sponsees, and running. As I dug my way out of the financial mess I got myself in, God's grace blessed me all along the way. As my life unfolded, I developed my relationship with the Lord. I knew that since I let go of the idea of getting married and having a family at thirty-eight, I was going to have to improvise. I had seen my cousin Grace when she was visiting in Nantucket, and still, all these years later, despite all the ups and downs of life, we were the happiest when we were together. The job with Legal Sea Food was still wonderful, but I didn't have anything that was keeping me tied to Boston. We talked about the idea of me coming out to California to live. I mean, why not? I was enjoying my job, but I was certainly open to a new adventure, a new beginning to the next exciting decade of my life. Another added blessing was that since I probably wouldn't have children, I could be around her children. My niece and nephew loved their Aunt Coffee Cup (one of the sweet nicknames they had for me), and I would feel as though I was a part of a family experience. I had plenty of opportunity to find work in California. I said I would think about it.

When I got back from Nantucket, I got a call from my friend Jeffrey, the one who picked me up at Grace's when I was angry about her telling me the truth about George. He had moved back to the East Coast and was visiting his mom. His dad had passed away since our last visit in San Francisco. I loved how he was taking care of his mother, which was very much like how I took care of my mother. I took my mom on trips, and he had just returned from taking his mom to Maine. Spiritually, we were both raised Catholic, we had a desire to have a deeper relationship with God, and we worked toward it. He loved to share with me his dating stories. Interestingly enough, he had been on a redhead kick (What was I? Chopped liver?). He said he was going to be in Waltham, and asked if I would like to meet up for dinner. Of course, I said yes! I wore a little black sundress. We went to The

Chalet, a restaurant in Waltham. As we drove over, I felt so comfortable with Jeff, combined with butterflies. It was effortless. He was funny and chatty, telling me about his golfing and a little background on the friends he was introducing me to. When we arrived, everyone was at the bar. They were so fun, and we laughed and ate, and I listened to stories of when they all lived together. They were family living life together, through thick and thin. I so admired the friendship, love, and loyalty. The night seemed to fly by. We ended up playing pool at the end of the night. I didn't want it to end.

I told Jeff I was considering moving to California and that it was an exciting option for me. I was ready for a change, and nothing was holding me in Massachusetts. Why not? At the end of the night, he drove me home and walked me to my door. He came in to pick up his things, and then it happened. The long-awaited KISS! Oh, I couldn't believe it was happening. I was flooded with emotions. We were such good friends, "best friends," according to him. I believed (here's that ugly word "delusional") he knew what it meant to make an advance. As he was getting ready to leave, he said, "I don't know if we should have done this. You're my best friend, and I don't want to hurt you." I assured him that we would always be friends, that even if he decided not to pursue a romantic involvement, we would remain friends. I knew, or should I say, I wanted to believe, that he would be floating on love like I was. We kissed goodnight and I was filled with excitement and possibility!

The next day I went to bring coffee to my best friend Shuby. I walked into Starbucks, and the song playing was "At Last," by Etta James. The lyrics say, "At last my love has come along," and they held every thought and emotion I was feeling! My eyes welled with joy and elation. I believed God had blessed me with the love of my life because I was faithful to Him, and He wouldn't want me to settle. I took our coffee and went to tell her every detail of the night! She seemed skeptical, but Shuby always brings "real" to the excitement! I floated through that Sunday. I didn't hear from him, but that was okay as I knew I would. Monday came, and I went about my usual schedule—morning AA meeting, then work—with a glow on my face and skip in my step. At the end of the day, I came home and went out for my run (I was still training for the Boston Marathon). When I got home, the phone rang. It was him! My smile was from ear to ear.

"Hi, Red!" We chit-chatted and then . . . "Red, I can't do this! You're my best friend, and I don't want to lose our friendship."

I FELT LIKE THE WIND GOT KNOCKED OUT OF ME! He went on to say that it was such a good idea to go to California. I would love it there. He wanted to talk about my plans, but I was in shock. I told him I couldn't process this with him. I had to go. He asked when we could talk again, and I told him I would let him know when I was ready. As I hung up the phone, I turned to the cross over my bed and said out loud, "That wasn't funny!" I was devastated. How could he kiss me if he didn't think he was going to move forward with a relationship? Jeff knew me so well, or so I believed, that this almost seemed cruel. But I knew him better than that. He just didn't want me.

I cried myself to sleep, and the next day, I got up, hungover from the emotions of the night before. I knew I had to go to my morning AA meeting. That was my routine. I so wanted to share about my heartache, but I have been taught to share only the message of hope, not the mess. I was sharing on the reading, and at the end of the meeting, a new woman to sobriety approached me and asked if she could get my phone number. God prompted me to set up a coffee date with her on Wednesday, and I did. I went to work and told my colleagues the story, and we all just moved on into the activities of the day. I so wanted to just nestle into a BIG self-pity party for just me. I asked Shuby if I could come over on Friday and watch movies, eat popcorn, and bring my tissues so I could cry about the love that was lost before it began. As the days unfolded in the week, I did what was in front of me to do. When I met the new woman for coffee on Wednesday and listened to her story, and as I was sharing my experience of strength and hope, I realized I wasn't thinking about me. Service is a funny thing. It's the last thing my heart wants to do when I'm consumed with myself, but it is the only thing that takes me out of myself so I can move through my pain without realizing it.

I continued to run my miles for training, go to meetings, and meet with women after the meeting, and by the time Friday came, I had no desire to sit around and have a pity party. I was going to be just fine. That weekend, I went to a movie that came out in the theaters called The Story of Us with Bruce Willis and Michelle Pfiefer. It was a story of a couple who were getting a divorce, so they dropped their children at camp so they could work out the details. They both loved each other, but they had drifted from the core of their love and allowed life to distance them from the love they so passionately had for one another. At the end of the movie, the woman realizes that he was the one that shared all of her most important life moments and was the unexpected joy in the dial tone of life. She loved that he knew when she got up in the morning that she liked it quiet until after her first cup of coffee, and that he always knew how to make her laugh and brought out the fun in her and in their life. She didn't want to end the marriage; she wanted to grow together in it. It's a beautiful story of lifelong love. I cried at the end of the movie. Sobbed is a better word. I thought, I'm thirty-eight years old. I will NEVER have that. Someone who knows who I am, the core of me. I cried all night long, feeling the hopelessness of my situation. I was never going to have that in my life.

When I woke up the next day, I did what I always do. I went to my AA meeting, and after the meeting, I don't know if it was my morning devotion with the Lord or the hope shared in the meeting of God doing the impossible (getting sober was a miracle), but when I got in my car, I felt like I had a message from Jesus: "I'm the one who has been with you through it all." He was with me in the 3:00 AM panic when I was drinking and didn't know where I was and in the grief of the loss of my brother that no person could console. The encouragement and hope that would arrive in a phone call or a check, out of nowhere, at just the right time, for just the right amount . . . these are the million and one moments that develop a relationship built on faith and trust! He's always been there. I didn't need anyone because, in ALL of those moments, it was God—no parent, sibling, friend, or boyfriend can meet me, comfort me, and make the miraculous happen. Only God . . . full stop. My job now was to foster that relationship in more of an intentional way. He had the plans for me; I would follow them.

As the autumn unfolded, I took a trip to California to visit my cousin Grace, and she and her husband asked again if I would like to move there. This time, I said yes without hesitation. I would get to be around my sweet niece and nephew. My cousin is my favorite person in the world to be around, and I knew God was giving me another chance to live a life, happy, joyous and free!

Jeff would call periodically, and as God would have it, I never had answered the phone. They were always voice messages. He would say things like, "Maybe we ought to see if we could date?" It was definitely messages of a man who did not know what he wanted. I knew God was transitioning me to something big. So at Christmas, I drove to my mom's house in

Amsterdam, New York, and I got the phone call from the company my cousin's husband ran. They said they had a position for me in marketing and that I would have an interview over the phone after Christmas. I was thrilled. Those are the Christmas presents only God can give. What a fun adventure. Because I was referred by the CEO of the company, built my career on sales and marketing, and knew the corporate climate of a business, I felt pretty confident that I had a good shot at getting the job. The new year came, and I was filled with electric anticipation of what the year would bring. The interview went well, and they said that they would get back to me with the date for me to fly out for the formal introductions.

I had told my boss that I was going to be leaving within the month, and I would let her know what that would look like. During this time, I got a call from my old VP of Operations. He was part owner of a small inn and restaurant with banquet space. He felt confident on managing the financials as well as the restaurant management side, but he didn't have a lot of experience with the inn. He brought one of his old Food and Beverage Managers from the restaurant group and wanted me to come down and see the inn and have dinner at the restaurant. I told him my plans, but he said to come down anyhow, so I did.

It was in the most adorable town, with a Currier and Ives type of feel. Everything I would ever want, if I were married. The inn needed work, but was in a fabulous location right on the harbor. The dining room was all glass, sitting on the water with an amazing view of the harbor. When I was seated in the dining room of the restaurant, I could not believe what I was seeing. Out there on the water, with a floodlight shining directly on it, was a lobster boat named Kathleen. Coincidence? I thought it was so interesting and something I would normally take as a sign from God that this opportunity was something to be strongly considered. No, no, although it would be such an exciting challenge, it was the wrong timing, and I was going to California!

I told Jim I couldn't take the job, but I would come and see him on Saturday and help him put a corporate strategy together. He said he would look forward to it. This was Wednesday night, and I was sure I would hear something about my new job in California. When Friday came, I got a voicemail message at work, but it wasn't from the new company. It was Jeff. His message was not wish-washy like it had been in his past voicemails. He was a lot more confident, almost bold in his message. He said for the sake of our friendship, or at least our history in AA, would I call him back and at least hear him out. I thought, well this actually sounds like a man who knows what he wants. I didn't think about it, I just called. It sounded like I took him by surprise, and he asked if he could see me. He said he wanted to tell me what he had discovered about himself, and that if after I heard him out, I didn't want to see or hear from him, that would be fine, but he needed to know if we had something. Wow, where was this message three months ago? Anyhow, I was going to California, so it would be the right thing to do to meet up.

We set up a visit for Sunday at a Starbucks that had a fireplace in Burlington, Massachusetts. I couldn't believe I was going to see him. I could make my amends and leave with our friendship repaired. I was curious what he had to say, and my heart still fluttered thinking about it, but I had my plans, and I was glad I would leave well.

When I got home on Friday, the phone rang, and it was Human Resources in California for my new job. She apologized for taking so long to get back to me, but she wanted to let me know that they had already filled the position that I applied for. No one took it down off of the server, and so they thought it was still available. What? I was stunned! How could this be? "God, what's happening right now? Wednesday you give me a dream job that's mine for the taking, then a call from Jeffrey, and now this?"

I needed to let this settle. "God, what are you up to?" I knew if I wanted to go to California, I could get another job out there, but I needed to just play this all out and keep an open mind. I had the appointment with Jim at the hotel the next day. I loved the idea of working there. Like I told Jim the night I saw the property, this would be a dream job, but as a single person it would be tough. I would rather be thirty-eight and single in California than in this adorable, sleepy, little town surrounded with families with 2.5 kids, all the things I wanted but had accepted were not going to be my future. When I got to the inn, Jim and I chatted, and we went over plans and strategies. I explained to him what had happened with Jeff, and told him that if Jeff says what I think he's going to say, then I would love to take the job. If not, then I would plan to still go to California. I should know by Monday, and Jim said no problem.

Sunday came, and I was heading to the Starbucks. It was a long morning in prayer, journaling, quiet. I wanted to be calm and present for our meeting. I knew I would pray when I got there, so I would speak God's message, not mine. I didn't want to manipulate or try to get him to say things that I wanted to hear but that he wasn't feeling. When I saw him, it took my breath away. I was nervous but calm. I knew God was with me, and this felt like a divine appointment. We hugged and exchanged hellos and got our coffee. We sat down and nestled in for a long chat. Before we got started, I went into the bathroom and asked God to be with me, with us, and be the narrator of this story.

When I went out to sit, Jeff asked if he could go first. He said that he was confused this summer and that he thought he was going to lose something that meant too much to him, our friendship. But in reality, he did just that. He told me how he talked with his friends, and they all thought he made a mistake in not being willing to try to have a relationship with me. On one of his visits with his friends, he shared how he was driving back from Cape Cod, and he went to see a friend of his. He meandered back as he couldn't remember exactly where he lived, but when he got to the town he lived in, he fell in love with it. When he got back to his mother's house, he told her he found the place he wanted to live. I was crying when he told me this because I just knew he was talking about Cohasset where the hotel was. He saw my tears, and said, "You're moving, aren't you?" I asked him what the name of the town was. He said, "Cohasset." My heart stopped!

God could not have been more clear in His direction of the U-turn of my life. I shared with Jeff everything that happened to me in the past five days, and it was truly a remarkable story. But God! All that I thought I knew and all my plans. How could this be? I knew that I knew one thing above everything, that no matter how much I loved this man, and I did love him, God was my source of supply. Not Jeffrey. I wouldn't have received that powerful understanding if the story hadn't unfolded the way it did. I was raised, as I think most of us are, thinking that the man will be the provider. My old ideas are ingrained in me. Even if we are both working, it will still be Him I rely upon. God had to work on us both if we were going to have a relationship that honored God first, our recovery, family, and faith. He had all the details orchestrated, and then He brought us into the fold. I love our God! In the next nine months, we began our romantic relationship, I started the job at the Inn on Cohasset Harbor, I ran the Boston Marathon, we got engaged on Mother's Day, and we married October 27, 2001! It was everything I could have hoped or imagined true love would feel like! All the whispers of my heart unfolded for the next chapter of my life!

Our wedding day was the happiest day of my life. I couldn't believe it was real. We had a wonderful rehearsal dinner at the Inn. All the out-of-town guests and family were there. We had a clambake, and it was just a beautiful evening. The next day I went to the beach at Scituate and watched the sun rise while thanking God for this amazing blessing of a lifetime. I prayed for my soon-to-be husband and our life together. I prayed that we would follow His will for us, as a couple and individually. My cousin rented a house on the water, so I went to get her so we could go get coffee and get ready for the blessed day! Hair and make-up and hanging at the salon. Such a beautiful time. Off we went to get dressed, but first a quick drive, just Grace and I, listening to Bette Midler "Going to the Chapel." I was so grateful to have her my whole life. It was one of those moments that you could only share with that one person who knew all the many sides of you.

My mother walked me down the aisle, and I was so grateful to have had her to share this precious moment in my life and hers. I know it was a blessing for her to see me walk down the aisle to a man she knew would take good care of me for the rest of my life. I wore her wedding dress. I had it altered to a strapless with gauntlet sleeves. The bustle and train remained the same. We married in the Catholic Church, primarily for our mothers. My soon-to-be pastors were at the wedding, and I was so grateful that they came.

They couldn't stay for the reception, but I was blessed to meet them shortly after we got back from our honeymoon.

Our reception was a ball! The food was cooked to perfection, filet and scallops, and the pièce de résistance—coconut cake with coconut frosting accompanied with individual hot fudge. Oh, my goodness, so yummy! When it was time to move the tables for dancing, my Director of Food and Beverage said that if this was me sober, he would be frightened to see what I was like drinking.

Jeff and I left that evening and stayed at the airport Hilton as we had an early flight the next day. We went to San Francisco for two nights and then on to Hawaii. Maui and Kauai, convertible, amazing food and beaches. It was the time of my life. We stopped back in California and spent a night at my cousin's beautiful bungalow in Pebble Beach. It was like a dream, way beyond what I could have hoped or imagined. God's abundant love showered down on us as we entered into our new life together as husband and wife!

Chapter 25

NEW LIFE

I felt like life was too good to be true. I loved working with Jim, and being married was so comfortable, almost as though we had always been together. When we got back from paradise, Jeff took me to his church where he got baptized. I was excited to meet his pastors, John and Lori Hatcher. Their church was in Weymouth, Massachusetts, and was ironically called New Life Foursquare Church. When we entered the church, it was not what I was used to physically. Raised Catholic, I expected stained glass, statues of saints, a crucifix—you get the idea. This was a building that had a stage and banquet chairs, with very simple accents, but it felt different—warm, with the presence of the Holy Spirit heavy on the place. The service started with worship music. I wept and didn't understand why. Later I learned that the tender space of worshiping the Lord is where the presence of the Holy Spirit is the strongest.

Pastor John and Lori have four children, and their oldest girl, Emily, was on stage singing. She sang a song that took me to my knees: "The Alabaster Box." Cece Winans sings a beautiful version. It is the story of Mary Magdalene. I feel like I am the modern-day version of the story in Luke 7:36-50. I was moved by the lyrics: "You weren't there the night He found me, you did not feel what I felt when He wrapped His loving arms around me. You don't know the cost of the oil in my alabaster box!"

I wanted to follow Jesus in a way like I never had before. I saw the love of Jesus alive in the way these people were living out their lives. The song said it all. He saved me, my whole life. I saw such a beautiful light inside this community that I had never experienced. They were living a pure and authentic life that called to me. I learned much in AA, but this was a whole other level of living a life for God. I wasn't comfortable with talking about Jesus. I had such a distortion of people who lived for Jesus and what a life of Christianity looked like. The reality was it looked like this sixteen-year-old young lady singing about the love she had for Jesus. I found it so admirable that she was not ashamed in the least for who she was and who she loved!

I found out so much about this beautiful family and the other families that were part of the church. Pastor John was Irish and came from alcoholism. His father was saved in a powerful way and got right into ministry. John was then raised as a Christian. Pastor John brought the Bible to life and made it applicable to the issues of today. He talked in his sermons of the troubles he struggled with: anger, fear, ego! I couldn't get enough of what I was learning. My sweet husband gave me my first Bible, and it was a Life Application Bible that had an explanation of the scriptures below. Pastor John gave me hope that I could live out life carrying the light of Jesus in me.

Each week I grew in an understanding of what it was like to have a friend in Jesus, to have the love of the Father, and to be guided by the Holy Spirit. I thought I understood the Trinity, but I didn't in a personal way. The Catholic Church taught about an intercessor to take your sins to the Father. The idea that I could have this direct, personal relationship was on a plane of reality which I hadn't comprehended. I understood that my journey through the Twelve Steps brought me from a faith in God to a relationship with God, but I still struggled with the relationship with Jesus. I guess it was tied to prejudices from my upbringing. There was such freedom in this community to show their love and praise for our Lord. I was very reserved, with the awful fear of what others would think of me; self-centered fear had me in its grips. I would continue to grow in confidence and worship with raised hands and tears streaming down my cheeks. I left every service touched by a love that was a feeling that I couldn't manufacture from anything of this world.

Jeff had been laid off from his company, and he got a new job in Watertown, New York. Yikes, back to Upstate New York. He had no idea what he was in for. I was excited about our new adventure. I was tired; the hotel and the banquets were taking their toll on me. It was the opportunity to actually have some time off. Wow, what a concept. But I was going to have to leave my church. I decided that I wanted to get baptized before we left for New York, so I arranged with Pastor John and Lori to have the baptism in Pastor

Jerry and Alice Fahey's pool. I wore a lovely dress to the Faheys, then I changed into my swimsuit with a peach cover up. I brought the "white linen" dress for after (which I totally felt was appropriate for anyone that was going to be washed clean— what an ego. Ugh). It was a beautiful ceremony surrounded by my beautiful church families, and of course my wonderful husband. When it was time for me to come in to get changed, Pastor Jerry looked pale. Um, your dress. Well, our dog peed on it! God has such an amazing sense of humor. Sweet Pastor Jerry was frantically trying to remove the stain before the service was over but to no avail. I believe the Lord had the prank orchestrated. I left the Faheys with a huge smile on my face, humbled by my God and grateful for this life-altering experience!

God took us to Sackets Harbor to live in an adorable house right on Lake Ontario. It was a gift to the both of us and our marriage, as we had been so entrenched in our life in AA, the work, the family, and friends; now it was just the two of us. It was a precious time for us to settle into our marriage. We tried to find a church that felt like New Life, but we struggled finding the feeling of home. We got involved at St. Andrew Catholic Church, and I volunteered for Sunday School. I helped out in the kitchen as well. It was a lovely little community, and I enjoyed my time there, but I have to say we did not feel like we were fed on the Word like we were at New Life.

The beautiful time we had away from the business of life provided such a perfect environment to focus on having a family. Jeff and I were trying to have children naturally, but we were older. I was thirty-nine and he was forty-two. I was working for a lovely, amazingly creative woman who had a bakery and a restaurant in the little town of Sackets Harbor. Everyone got their pastries at the bakery, and the restaurant was always full. She was a talented chef. I offered to work in catering with her and her best friend Kris. We had a ball. Cheryl would get the business, and we would execute it. We saw some beautiful estates on the Thousand Islands and locally. It was a sweet season. When it was over, about a year and half later, Jeff got laid off. We were grateful for the season but knew we had to get back to Massachusetts, and so, just like that, I left Sackets Harbor, New York to get a job as a waitress at Legal Sea Foods in Braintree, Massachusetts, where I lived with my wonderful mother-in-love, Rosemary.

She was such a gift. Not only was I her daughter-in-love, we were great friends. We would chat away the hours; we were blessed to have this "girly time" together. She had an amazing gift of making me feel seen, appreciated, and like her friend. I treasured our time together.

I loved waitressing! I loved serving my guests and always trying to anticipate their needs. This would lead to wonderful interaction and conversation that would always be unsuspecting and usually delightful. One day as I was working at the restaurant, I had a table of four lovely ladies who were just vibrant, engaging, gracious, and funny. We hit it off immediately, and I found out they worked for the Massachusetts Department of

Social Services. I told them how Jeffrey and I were trying to have children, but it wasn't happening naturally. They explained that they were in the Foster Care/Adoption side of DSS, and I should consider adopting through the State. I explained I had hoped that we could adopt babies, and they told me it was a myth that you can't get a baby through the State. We continued to explore all options for building a family. As we both found employment, I began working in sales for HealthSouth Radiology. I solicited doctors in the Boston area to utilize MRI and CT services at our free-standing facility. It was a wonderful job, and I worked for a beautiful woman, inside and out, from church. It couldn't have been a better partnership. I had a great healthcare package, which helped as we explored if I was still even capable of having children at this point. We went to the top Sack doctor at MassGeneral. He did the tests, and the only thing I was open to was the Follicle Stimulation hormone. I knew that I would not do well with Invitro, and we both felt there are too many children we could adopt that it just seemed our natural plan B. The result was, there were no eggs to stimulate. That was it; there was not going to be a natural birth. I had to let that sink in for a hot minute. I was disappointed, to say the least. Fortunately, I had enough healing from the guilt from my abortions that, although I struggled with the thoughts that I was being punished, I knew that I was not. That was another fiery dart from the enemy that said God's forgiveness doesn't mean anything, which is a lie straight from the pit of hell. Once forgiven, always forgiven.

I felt like God blessed me with mercy to even consider being a mother. There were so many children that needed love and a good home. I knew God would grace us with the ability to provide that. I didn't wait to vacillate about our plan B. Time was literally ticking. I set appointments to be interviewed for international adoption and domestic adoption. It just didn't feel like it was the right fit. I was praying to God and asked where were we to go to build our family? Then I remembered my sweet table of angels at Legal Sea Food. Foster Care was His response! God has a beautiful plan, and He orchestrates all the details so that when you're ready to move the way He wants you to move, it unfolds under grace in perfect and easy ways.

We reached out to the Adoption division of the Department of Social Services. We received a call back with a plan for moving forward. I knew my baby was coming. I felt all the blocks of the other paths we explored close as the Foster Care Adoption journey flowed easily, under grace in perfect and easy ways. That's how God shows me I'm in His will. I knew He had knitted a family together for us and that the shame and self-condemnation had no place here. I asked for forgiveness, and I have a Merciful Father. In order to begin the journey of a family, with all the plans He had for the children He would entrust to us, He wanted me to accept His forgiveness completely. Were we ready? Of course, we were!

Chapter 26

THE SOUND OF SCREECHING BRAKES

The sound of screeching brakes and the honk of the horn caused me to snap out of the swirl of what I had going on in my head. Startled, my instincts kicked in and I swerved, coffee in hand, the car stopping inches away from me.

In Boston rush hour traffic, there is no room for indecision. Forget what the crosswalk light shows. RUN. Jaywalking was commonly practiced in the city, and, as you know by now, fits perfectly with my spirit of not following the rules. Then there's the maze of one-way streets, turnabouts, and drivers who think they are Mario Andretti (I am definitely one of them). It is moments like this that confirm again God's grace alive in the moments of my life, His blanket of protection around the little redhead, even as the enemy was at large. Especially that morning. God's angels were dressed for battle in front of the Courthouse. Redemption was not going to be stolen this rainy morning!

It was a morning of mixed emotions as my husband and I poured our hearts out to the Lord for grace and favor. The unfolding of the morning was riddled with fear and answered with faith. Our fate was in the courtroom we were getting ready to enter. It was our Abraham and Isaac walk up the mountain, the moment the knife is raised.

I continued on to the entrance of the courthouse where I would wait for my husband to meet me after he parked the car. As my heart slowed down after the adrenaline left my body, I gathered myself and took a long deep breath. I looked down to assess the damage. Fully prepared for my pretty, light blue dress to have been splattered with coffee, a sigh of relief flowed through me as not a drop was spilled from my uncovered cup of coffee (the secret is using my arm like a hydraulic system). One less thing to feel stressed about (God's grace alive in the tiniest of details that brings peace and confirms He's got this). I never have a top on my coffee! The covers have too small a hole for this caffeine addict, and as I drink my coffee black, it is way too hot and burns my mouth. However, one of the hazards of an open cup of coffee is spillage. Oh, the outfits I have ruined, and why is it always white or light colors that seem to have the worst mishaps?

My husband walked up to the Courthouse entrance to meet me (he looks so handsome in his blue suit, gold tie, the love of my life). He had witnessed the whole thing.

"Wow, Red, that was amazing. A near-death experience, and you didn't spill a drop. Impressive." He looked at me and said, "Are you ready for our next adventure?" Then he took my hand, and we walked into the courthouse. We were ready to take on the untraditional challenge of bringing about the family that God had already designed before we were born. We had God on our side, and we believed it was His purpose for us to adopt this precious angel. With Christ ALL things are possible!

As we walked through the metal detectors, I thought about the fact that I was a woman who epitomized a modern-day Mary Magdalene. I had been controlled by alcohol and drugs and made decisions which caused chaos, heartbreak, pain and even death. I used to cry out that "I couldn't take care of myself, how could I take care of someone else?" That same person was now, by God's grace, redeemed to be considered "capable" enough to be a mother. Only God, through His love, could restore what the locusts had eaten.

If you feel hopeless; as though you can't change, or the pain is too much, if you can't seem to stop using a substance or stop the cycle of self-pity, if you are unable to control your emotional nature and feel it would be easier if you just didn't wake up. If this is you, and you've read to this point in my book, it's time to say this simple prayer:

Dear Heavenly Father,

I believe that you loved me so much that you sent your Son to carry the cross for my sins. I know I have sinned and have been trying to become a better person on my own, but I can't do it. Please forgive me. I can't in my own will-power stop the pain. I've tried over and over again. But I know that Jesus can, and I'm asking Him into my heart and my life. I will live the rest of my days getting to know You, Jesus, and developing my relationship with You through your Word, the Bible. Thank you, Father, for saving me because you love me and want to know me. I am Yours!

Amen

This will be the best decision you can ever make. Your next step is to write down the whispers of your heart. Put down all that you want your life to be. Find a place to put it (I have a God Box to keep my prayers, hopes and desires in), and open it up a year from now. You will be amazed at the miracles God has materialized in your life! I know I was!

"The Lord bless you and keep you
The Lord make His face shine upon you
and be gracious to you
The Lord turn His face toward you
and give you peace."

Numbers 6:24-26

ACKNOWLEDGMENTS

First, I want to thank God for His grace in my life! Thank You for unconditionally loving me and forgiving the unforgivable. Thank You for blessing me with the whispers of my heart. Thank You for the beauty You surround me with. From the ashes of my life decisions and alcoholism, You brought purpose and meaning. Thank You for your mercies that are fresh every day!

I want to thank my beautiful cousin Penny Bradley (cheerleader, confidante, mentor, partner in crime), who has been my greatest life-long gift. Without your belief in me and your example of thoughtfulness and generosity, your sense of humor, and your unconditional love, I would not have had a willingness to survive. You make me want to strive harder to be better. You are the wings beneath my feet.

Shuby, without your awareness and encouragement, I might never have gotten sober. Your friendship has blessed my life through your generosity, authenticity, creative lens of life, and unconditional love. Thank you for being there when it mattered most.

Lori Hatcher, God called me to you! First for mentoring me as a new Christian, then taking my hand as I said YES to the Lord when He first said, "Tell them of My grace alive in your life! It will give them hope." Thank you for your love for Jesus and the way you walk it out in your family and how you've blessed mine!

Darcy Regan, I can't imagine where I would be, or where my relationships would be, without your steady sponsorship. You have loved me so well as you've consistently brought me back to the truth: "Either God is everything, or He's nothing. What is your choice to be?" Thank you for your effervescent spirit and for showing me what a big, beautiful life in recovery looks like!

Thank you to my coach, mentor, and inspiration—award-winning author Missy Maxwell Worton—a warrior who lovingly encouraged me through the process of healing required to get this book written. My book and the many books of the Warrior Writers that have been already or will be written for kingdom impact would not have been penned without her obedience to the Lord and her YES! The Warrior Writers has blossomed into a full service publishing company, and my Warrior Sisters and I have had the privilege of gleaning from her example and wisdom.

Thank you to Ashley Hagan, my AMAZING editor. You graciously kept my voice while directing and correcting my story with respect, love, and professionalism! It has been an honor to work with you, and I look forward to many more books and projects along the way.

Thank you to all of the friends and family, old and new, along the way. Your touch in my life is what has brought me through this journey.

Thank you to my parents and brothers for your unconditional love! Thank you for always seeing the best in me and forgiving my unacceptable behavior. Your sacrifice, generosity, traditions, and constant support blessed me with a foundation from which to grow from.

Lastly, thank you to the love of my life and my sweet boys! So much to say . . . a whole other book can be written!

Jeffrey, it was always you! I'm so grateful to God for your amazing heart, character, generosity, kindness, and unconditional love! "Lucy . . . you got some splainin' to doooooo!" I love doing life with you!

My Nicholas and Chad, thank you for your unconditional love and for filling my life with a love that I never knew possible! Your ability to show grace and forgiveness to me as I've stumbled through mothering you has taught me more than I ever thought possible. I love you both to eternity and back.

Original artwork by Nicholas Alan Janson

The above picture displays my son Nicholas' talent, but more than that, it shows his heart! I have always made a big deal decorating for my sons' birthdays, and on my birthday two years ago, Nicholas woke up before I did (that's early!) and decorated the kitchen with flowers, signs, and balloons, and this drawing was his gift! It was the book cover I had described to him. Although we ultimately went a different direction with the cover, I want to thank you, Nicholas, for one of my greatest gifts, other than you making me a Mother!

About the Author

KATE JANSON is an author, speaker, and life coach. She has worked in the hospitality business her whole career, from managing hotels to running an international event planning company, as well as a catering business. She has worked with women in recovery from alcohol and drug addiction for 30 years. Kate has been saved by God's grace from her own broken road of alcohol and substance addiction, and she wants to share the hope of Jesus—the forgiving grace that is needed to be healed.

For more, find her at www.godsgraceinalife.com.